Hope
for
Europe

66 Propositions
by
Thomas Schirrmacher

Foreword
by
Frank Hinkelmann

ISBN 978-3-933372-48-2

© 2002, Thomas Schirrmacher / VTR Publications, 1st ed.
© 2018, Thomas Schirrmacher / VTR Publications, 2nd amended ed.

VTR Publications,
Gogolstr. 33, 90475 Nürnberg, Germany
http://www.vtr-online.com

Translation: Cambron Teupe
Editing: Esther Waldrop

Photo credit:
European Parliament, Author: dinamicline, Wikimedia Commons
https://commons.wikimedia.org/wiki/File:European_Parlament_-_
panoramio_(1).jpg

"And now these three remain: faith, hope and love.
But the greatest of these is love."
(1 Corinthians 13:13)

"But sanctify the Lord God in your hearts:
and be ready always to give an answer
to every man that asketh you a reason of the hope
that is in you with meekness and fear."
(1 Peter 3:15)

"For I know the plans I have for you, declares the LORD,
plans to prosper you and not to harm you,
plans to give you hope and a future."
(Jeremiah 29:11)

"Hope is to human existence what oxygen is for the lungs.
Without oxygen, the patient dies from asphyxiation.
Without hope, one suffers from the suffocation of despair,
the paralysis of one's spiritual vigor due to a feeling of nothingness,
of the absurdity of life."
(Emil Brunner)

Contents

Hope in the Face of Doomsday Speculation............................46

Hope for All Areas of Life 52

Hope for Europe
And what Christians have to do with it

Exactly 25 years ago, the then General Secretary of the European Evangelical Alliance and representatives of various European mission organisations came together to consider how spiritual renewal could become possible in Europe. One of the participants summarised how things developed in this way:

"During our conversation, God put on our hearts, above all, the three terms FAITH, HOPE and LOVE from 1 Corinthians 13. FAITH is a term which has an important meaning for committed Christians, but is considered by outsiders to be too pious. About LOVE much is said and sung, but often in a way that does not in any way honour God. HOPE, on the other hand, is a word much used in our time. People are looking for hope in economics and in politics. Where is the hope for the Balkans, for our young people, for old people? Thus the term 'Hope for Europe' was born." (Peter Regez)

Many discussions and consultations followed, the network grew bigger and bigger, and in spring 2002 the first congress of Christian European networks took place in Budapest under the motto "Hope 21 – Hope for the 21st Century", with more than 1,000 participants. A second congress followed in 2011.

From the very outset it was important to those responsible that all thinking about hope for Europe be based on a biblical-theological foundation. This theological basis was drawn up by the current chairman of the Theological Commission of both the World Evangelical Alliance and the European Evangelical Alliance, Thomas Schirrmacher.

In the meantime 25 years have passed. Europe has changed, not only because of the refugee flows of 2015 but first and foremost because of a fundamental political change of climate. The hopes that many had associated with a united and free Europe have given way to fears and insecurity, which in many cases have opened the door to populism and nationalism right into the heart of government. Instead of hope, pessimism prevails in many cases today, and fear shapes the social climate.

This pessimism was not limited solely to evangelical circles in all parts of Europe but as Schirrmacher aptly writes in thesis 2 of this book "Hope is typical for Christians" and further "Hope creates real future" (thesis 7). These two examples show that the author's 66 theses have lost none of their relevance, and that it is perhaps even more important today that Christians reappraise the biblical-theological basis of their hope.

In October 2018, another "Hope" conference will take place in Tallinn, Estonia, under the leadership of the European Evangelical Alliance. Once again, leading members of national Protestant Alliances, employees of Christian national and European networks, and representatives of Christian organisations will meet to work out together how Christians can be salt and light, and thus bring hope into our European society.

For this event, this valuable basic theological document, establishing a biblically founded hope, is being reissued.

It is my hope that this book on hope will contribute to a better and biblically founded understanding of hope.

Rev. Dr. Frank Hinkelmann
President of the European Evangelical Alliance

We Need Hope

"In my opinion, European integration offers immense
opportunities for missions, both a gift and a duty
given to our generation by the God of history.
With His assistance and under his wise Providence,
we can take advantage of these opportunities,
if we make the right decisions today."[1]

The following study has been composed for Hope for Europe, a joint agenda of the European Evangelical Alliance and the European branch of the Lausanne Movement, and is intended to serve as the basis of the first consultation of its Theology Commission at the Hope21 Conference in Budapest.

The study investigates the usage of the concept of 'hope' in the Old[2] and New Testament and considers the significance of these texts for us today (The Scriptures will be cited).

Each proposition will be thoroughly discussed from a biblical-theological point of view, and accompanied by an application relevant to our situation.

---

[1] Bernhard Knieß. "Die Chancen der europäischen Integration für die Mission". Evangelikale Missiologie 16 (2000) 4: pp. 122-133, here p. 122. The article contains recent data and important incentives for Christians in Europe.

[2] The Old Testament uses four verbs and one noun derived from one of their roots to designate the concept we call 'hope.'

1. Hope is Rational

Proposition: Hope is not a vague feeling based on opinions or expectations. God commands Christians to give account of our expectations: What do we hope, why, and how?[3]

Peter clearly expects the church to think its hopes through: "But in your hearts set apart Christ as Lord. Always be prepared to give an answer to everyone who asks you to give the reason for the hope that you have. But do this with gentleness and respect," (1 Pet. 3:15). Before giving account to others, we must first give account to ourselves. Hope does not contradict thought, and intensive thought will not destroy hope. Rather, deliberate, conscious consideration distinguishes between true hope and cheap comfort. As a result, Peter can speak of the reasons for our hope.[4]

Because our lives as Christians are to be changed by the renewal of our thinking (Rom. 12:2), we can find new hope only when we are prepared to surrender our old thought patterns for new ones. We must repeatedly ask the Holy Spirit to illuminate our reason. "I pray also that the eyes of your heart[5] may be enlightened in order that you may know the hope to which he has called you, the riches of his glorious inheritance in the saints" (Eph. 1:18), which means no less than the understanding of the Trinity, Father, Jesus Christ and the Spirit (Eph. 1:17) as God, "so that you may know him better." We study the Bible to win hope for ourselves as well as for our families, our churches and our society. "For everything that was written in the past was written to teach us, so that through endurance and the encouragement of the Scriptures we might have hope" (Rom. 15:4).

---

[3] In many languages, 'hope' means three different things: 1) the act of hoping. i.e., the content and manner of my expectations, 2) the object of hope, what I hope for, and 3) the person or thing which is to fulfill my hope. For Christians, therefore, it means 1) hope in our hearts, 2) hope for salvation, and 3) hope in God, who creates our salvation.

[4] Greek *logon peri tes elpidos*.

[5] In the Bible, the heart is the center of thought.

2. Hope is Typical of Christians; Faith and Hope Belong Together

Proposition: Hope is typical of Christians (Heb. 3:6; Eph. 4:4), for "faith is being sure of what we hope for and certain of what we do not see" (Heb. 11:1).

Thus hope is the elementary confession of every Christian, for "Let us hold unswervingly to the hope we profess, for he who promised is faithful" (Heb 10:23). The Bible constantly emphasises the close relationship between faith and hope, as do two examples from Peter and Paul. Speaking of Jesus, Peter says, "Through him you believe in God, who raised him from the dead and glorified him, and so your faith and hope are in God" (1 Pet. 1:21), and Paul reminds us that through Christ "we have gained access by faith into this grace in which we now stand. And we rejoice in the hope of the glory of God"(Rom. 5:2). Peter leaves no doubt that the new birth – the divine activity that makes us Christians – produces living hope: "Praise be to the God and Father of our Lord Jesus Christ! In his great mercy he has given us new birth into a living hope through the resurrection of Jesus Christ from the dead" (1 Pet. 1:3). Shouldn't our living hope be more visible to the world?

European Christians need to learn to confess their hope in all situations and to remind our churches that hope, not resignation, fear or concealment, is the emblem of our faith. Especially Evangelicals must proclaim that hope and rebirth are inseparable – not only in theory, but also in everyday life.

3. Hope Creates Unity

Proposition: It is hope that unites all Christians: Because "There is one body and one Spirit – just as you were called to one hope when you were called" (Eph. 4:4), Christians will never establish their unity without speaking of their common hope.

European Christians must unite in their hope and show the world that neither we, our church, nor our organisations constitute that hope, but the love and the grace of God made concrete in Jesus Christ. Anyone who attacks the unity of Christianity robs Europe of its hope.

4. Love Creates Hope; Hope Creates Love

Proposition: Love and hope are inseparable. For this reason, Paul can "remember before our God and Father your work produced by faith, your labour prompted by love, and your endurance inspired by hope in our Lord

Jesus Christ" (1 Thes. 1:3). Faith, hope and love are often mentioned together (1 Cor. 13:13; see also Col. 1:5 and Gal. 5:5-6). "Our Lord Jesus Christ himself ... who loved us and by his grace gave us eternal encouragement and good hope" (2 Thes. 2:16) is the love of God that produces the hope, for "hope does not disappoint us, because God has poured out his love into our hearts by the Holy Spirit, whom he has given us" (Rom. 5:5). This love which God gives us creates hope for others, for love "always protects, always trusts, always hopes, always perseveres" (1 Cor. 13:7).

As Jesus tells us, a society without hope and without the Law of God is cold and loveless. "Because of the increase of wickedness, the love of most will grow cold" (Matt. 24:12). Enmity against God's commandments is enmity against love. *No other scripture better describes modern Europe's basic problem. No one can repudiate God's laws of creation without repudiating love. We will never restore love to our families, our churches, our employment relationships, our society or our government until we return to the Law of God. Lawlessness always ends in lovelessness – as our present situation clearly demonstrates! Ever since the 60s, we speak of love more than ever before, while crime and hate continue to increase in all areas of life. Our society has forgotten what true love is! How can Europe relearn love when Christians neither teach nor live it?*

5. The Human Being Cannot Live without Hope

Proposition: Hope is essential to man's being. "Hope is to human existence what oxygen is for the lungs. Without oxygen, the patient dies from asphyxiation. Without hope, one suffers from the suffocation of despair, the paralysis of one's spiritual vigor due to a feeling of nothingness, of the absurdity of life" (Emil Brunner).[6]

European civilisation has never doubted this fact, even though many have sought their hope elsewhere than in the Father of Jesus Christ. Plato defined hope as "the expectation of something good,"[7] a definition of human existence. And what about the leftist philosopher Ernst Bloch, who wrote the influential book *The Principle Hope*?[8]

---

[6] Emil Brunner. op. cit., p. 7.

[7] Plato. *Definitiones* 416.

[8] Ernst Bloch. *Das Prinzip Hoffnung*. 3 Vols. Suhrkamp: Frankfurt, 1982 (Original 1954-1959, several reprints); *The Principle Hope*. Blackwell: Oxford, 1986.

The influence of hope can be seen in various European ideologies such as Marxism[9] or National Socialism[10]. Faith in the future achievements of such worldviews gives them immense influence and motivates people to dedicate their lives to them. New Age, Islam, youth sects, and political party programs all derive their power from their visions of the future. The Bible is no exception, but only its revelation is truth, for the One Who inspired Scripture is the One Who makes the future.

Hope, part of the dignity of man – the image of God – is both a human right and a birthright which all men owe to all others. That right is only surrendered when the individual refuses to believe in God. Every person has some conception of the future – in fact, according to the discipline of comparative religious studies, every religion has some explanation of future world history.

Anyone alive can hope and should do so (Ecc. 9:4), but the dead can no longer hope (Ecc. 4:5-6) unless their faith in God permits them to hope for the resurrection from the dead.[11]

6. Tomorrow Depends on Today

Proposition: Our expectations or hopes of the future determine how we act today. The present of every human being depends on his expectations for the future.

The Bible gives us sufficient examples of concrete admonitions, comfort and commandments for the present derived from the promises for the future. If we claim to be able to do without expectations for the future, we deceive ourselves, for we then automatically accept the views of our society. Unfor-

---

[9] See Thomas and Christine Schirrmacher "Der Kommunismus als Lehre vom Tausendjährigen Reich". Factum 11+12/1986: pp. 12-19 and Thomas Schirrmacher. Marxismus – Opium für das Volk?. Schwengeler: Berneck, 1990[1]; VKW: Bonn, 1997[2].

[10] See Thomas Schirrmacher. "Die Religion des Nationalsozialismus: 14 Dokumente". Factum 11/1989: pp. 506-510; ders. "Adolf Hitler und kein Ende: Ausgewählte neuere Literatur zur Geschichte und Vorgeschichte des Nationalsozialismus". Factum 6/1989: pp. 252-255; ders. 'Das göttliche Volkstum' und der 'Glaube an Deutschlands Größe und heilige Sendung': Hans Naumann im Nationalsozialismus". 2 Vols. VKW: Bonn, 1992[1]; 2000[2].

[11] See the proposition on the Resurrection.

tunately, many believers reflect the views of politicians and television more than biblical teaching. Our own pessimistic views of our own future, the future of our church, or of the world are also determined by certain views of the future, even though we cannot always define these ideas.

Since our views of the future play a significant role in our attitudes toward the immediate future, it is essential to ask whose view of reality is most accurate. When we fail to formulate concrete ideas, we leave the field to sects such as the Jehovah's Witnesses, who bank on their special eschatological systems. In fact, once you understand their eschatology, you understand their doctrine. The same can be said for many of the strange splitter groups which exist in Evangelical camps as well. We must find definite answers to such movements, even though we need to tolerate a certain amount of variation.

Questions about the future depend on the central issues of the Christian faith, such as the Second Coming of Christ, the Last Judgment, and the Resurrection of the Dead – issues inseparable from the nature and the office of Jesus. For this reason it is essential to distinguish between issues which the Bible clearly answers (that Jesus is coming back to judge all men), questions which Scripture answers only partially, and issues which Scripture ignores completely and which arise only when theologians insist on completing the system they have developed. Only such clarity in our teaching can stop the flood of false prophecy in Evangelical circles.

7. Hope Creates a True Future

Proposition: If God had not provided us with the future, we would have none. Only because He promises us the future, do we have a future. "So there is hope for your future," declares the LORD (Jer. 31:17).

This future is not merely a progression of time, but the heights and depths of history which lead to a final good future. "'For I know the plans I have for you,' declares the LORD, 'plans to prosper you and not to harm you, plans to give you hope and a future'" (Jer. 29:11). Anyone who takes the goal of history as his starting point and includes God's final judgment will reckon with a future authentic in quality as well as in quantity: "There is surely a future hope for you, and your hope will not be cut off" (Prov. 23:18).

8. Hope Is Not Cool Calculation, for It Reckons with Things Yet Invisible

Proposition: The strength of Christian hope is its belief and dependence on the invisible world. "Hope is nothing more than to depend on and wait for things one cannot see" (Martin Luther).

Luther derived this statement from the definition of faith in the Letter to the Hebrews. "Now faith is being sure of what we hope for and certain of what we do not see" (Heb 11:1). Paul adds, "For in this hope we were saved. But hope that is seen is no hope at all. Who hopes for what he already has? But if we hope for what we do not yet have, we wait for it patiently" (Ro 8:24-25).

It is just this quality which gives hope the transforming spiritually liberating power which non-Christians cannot understand.

The materialism we have seen in Western Europe in the last decades may present itself in a different form than in Eastern Europe, but its roots are the same. In a continent more forged by materialism than any other part of the world, where many only believe what they can see, people desperately need the message that true hope is to be found in an invisible God, and that true values come from within. European Christians could learn a lot from their brothers in the 'Two-Thirds World'.

Hope in God Alone Is Undeserved

9. Hope Depends on Grace, Not on Achievement

Proposition: The basis of our faith demonstrates clearly that all depends on God's grace and not on our achievements, for our achievements are the source of all that we can reckon and access, and these are simply insufficient for a true transformation.

As Martin Luther stated, "Hope does not come from our merits. Our merits come from hope." The doctrine of justification by faith, which Luther rediscovered, is the basis of a hope independent of merit: "so that, having been justified by his grace, we might become heirs having the hope of eternal life" (Tit. 3:7). Peter advises, "Set your hope fully on the grace to be given you when Jesus Christ is revealed" (1 Pet. 1:13), and other writers often mention hope in connection with grace (for example, 2 Thes. 2:6; Ps. 13:6; 130:7). Isaiah prays, "O LORD, be gracious to us; we long for you. Be our strength every morning, our salvation in time of distress" (Isa. 33:2).

10. Hope Cannot Be Earned

Proposition: Hope depends on grace and not on our piety or correct, superior theology, as much as we should endeavour to live and think in a godly way.

Eliphas, Job's friend, asks, "Should not your piety be your confidence and your blameless ways your hope?" (Job 4:6), but Job, in a hopeless state (Job 17:13, 15), has learned to set his hope on God alone.

When the Epistle to the Hebrews speaks of "the hope of which we boast" (Heb 3:6), and when Paul says, "we rejoice in the hope of the glory of God" (Rom. 5:2), they are not boasting of their own achievements but give God the glory and 'boast' in something they have in no way earned, and which is available to others as well.

Hope is, thus, just as much a gift of God as the object of our hope. Man can never 'earn' hope, for "hope only arises when God has mercy on us and pours it into our hearts" (Martin Luther). "Hope is based on God's pure, un-merited benevolence, which was promised out of grace, and is to be called upon by those who do not deserve it" (Martin Luther). A healthy optimism in a world of suffering, injustice, catastrophes and moral collapse is a gift of God, which all of us should pray for.

11. God Does Not Only Give Hope; He Is the Reason for Our Hope

Proposition: God does not only give us something to hope for. He is Him-self the essence of our hope. "But now, Lord, what do I look for? My hope is in you" (Ps. 39:7). The Psalms express this most clearly. "For you have been my hope, O Sovereign LORD, my confidence since my youth" (Ps. 71:5); "Find rest, O my soul, in God alone; my hope comes from him" (Ps. 62:5); "Blessed is he whose help is the God of Jacob, whose hope is in the LORD his God" (Ps. 146:5). The psalmist often associates hope with godliness (Ps. 33:18; 147:11; 62:6).

Only because we belong to God, and because He 'belongs' to us, can we hope at all. "I say to myself, 'The LORD is my portion; therefore I will wait for him'" (Lam. 3:24). We ought to sense that our hope lies not in ourselves, in our wonderful ideas or programs, or in our efforts and our fervour, but in God, the Giver of such ideas and fervour. Because He is the basis, the goal and the content of our hope, our hope continues even in the heavenly fulfilment of all promises, for Paul says, "And now these three remain: faith, hope and love. But the greatest of these is love" (1 Cor. 13:13), even when we see Jesus face to face (1 Cor. 13:12).

12. The Ungodly Have No Hope

Proposition: One of the Bible's most frequent statements on hope is that the ungodly have no true hope, only imagined, deceptive hope.

Paul reminds the Ephesians of their lives before they knew Christ: "At that time you were separate from Christ, excluded from citizenship in Israel and foreigners to the covenants of the promise, without hope and without God in the world" (Eph. 2:12) Unbelievers are "the rest of men, who have no hope" (1 Thes. 4:13). The logical conclusion for believers is not pride, but the urgent warning to trust God alone, for "Cursed is the one who trusts in man, who depends on flesh for his strength and whose heart turns away from the LORD" (Jer. 17:5).

Further Old Testament Scriptures

1 Chr. 29:15 "We are aliens and strangers in your sight, as were all our forefathers. Our days on earth are like a shadow, without hope."

Job 8:13 "Such is the destiny of all who forget God; so perishes the hope of the godless."

Job 7:6 "My days are swifter than a weaver's shuttle, and they come to an end without hope."

Job 8:13 "Such is the destiny of all who forget God; so perishes the hope of the godless."

Job 11:20 "But the eyes of the wicked will fail."

Job 19:10 "He tears me down on every side till I am gone; he uproots my hope like a tree."

Job 27:8 "For what hope has the godless when he is cut off, when God takes away his life?"

Ps. 37:9 "For evil men will be cut off, but those who hope in the LORD will inherit the land."

Prov. 11:7 "When a wicked man dies, his hope perishes; all he expected from his power comes to nothing."

Prov. 10:28 "The prospect of the righteous is joy, but the hopes of the wicked come to nothing."

Prov. 11:23 "The desire of the righteous ends only in good, but the hope of the wicked only in wrath."

13. Hope Without God Is Deceptive

Proposition: The Prodigal Son deceived himself when he placed his hopes on his friends. Once his money was spent, his friends disappeared as well. The hope he placed in his Father proved reliable, for it depended on love instead of on wealth (Lk. 15:11). How grateful we should be that the true Father in Heaven "loved us and by his grace gave us eternal encouragement and good hope" (2 Thes. 2:16).

Because "when a wicked man dies, his hope perishes; all he expected from his power comes to nothing" (Pr. 11:7), anyone can be disgraced and humiliated when he depends on men (Job 41:1). When one depends on other nations, one discovers that they cannot save (Lam. 4:17). When society collapses, "we look for justice, but find none" (Isa 59:11) and "We hoped for peace but no good has come" (Jer. 14:19; See also 2:37).

14. Hope Without God Must Find a Substitute in Creation

Proposition: Hope in God and faith and belief in Him can only be destroyed if a substitute can be found. As there is no other Creator outside Creation, this substitute can only be a part of Creation, be it idols, human beings, angels, nature or money.

The Fall demonstrates this clearly (Gen. 3:1, 7). In our modern 'neutral' mentality, Eve might have said to the serpent, "It is possible that God is not reliable and has not told us the truth. What about you? If I question God's word, you must allow me to also question you. I just cannot believe anyone at the moment, but just wait!" This conversation did not take place, of course, and could not have done so. Eve could abandon her trust in God only by believing the devil. She could not doubt God without believing something else. Neutrality cannot exist,[12] either in critical studies or in ethical decisions. Eve could not simply listen to both parties and then wait for results, for she had to continue to live, to act, and to decide. She could neither believe both nor obey both.

15. God Cannot Be Replaced as the Basis of Hope, Publicly or in Secret, as in the Religion of Mammon

Proposition: Any hope not finally based in God must prove deceptive, for it relies on something that cannot guarantee and that will itself one day fail.

Let us take a look at Europe's love of money and take notice of the consequences false hopes have for everyday life. In the Sermon on the Mount, Jesus said, "No one can serve two masters. Either he will hate the one and love the other, or he will be devoted to the one and despise the other. You cannot serve both God and Money" (Mt. 6:24; see also Lk. 16:13). Shortly before this, He had warned against spending our lives collecting treasures on earth, "for where your treasure is, there your heart will be also" (Mt. 6:21; see also Lk. 12:34). This was no new law, for the Old Testament and the New both criticise 'evil Mammon' (Lk. 16:9; the Greek word means either 'unjust' or 'evil'). The Bible protects private property (in the Ten Commandments, for example), bids us to work, and sometimes describes peace and prosperity as gifts of God, but when it emphasises that "the worker deserves his wages" (Lk. 10:7; see also 1 Tim. 5:18), that not only permits the labourer to enjoy his well-earned income, but also criticises those who fail to pay him for his work. James, the brother of Jesus, concurs: "Look! The wages you failed to pay the workmen who mowed your fields are crying out against you. The cries of the harvesters have reached the ears of the Lord Almighty" (Jas. 5:4; see also 5:1-6 and Dt. 24:15).[13]

---

[12] Heinrich Berger's summary of Calvin's view of history in Heinrich Berger: *Studien zur Dogmengeschichte und Systematischen* Theologie 6. Zwingli-Verlag: Zürich, 1956, p. 138 (See also pp. 138-139)

[13] Karl Marx's accusation of the Bible is absurd. Scripture was never intended to

No one who serves Mammon, Jesus tells us, can serve God at the same time. The Bible considers the love of money to be the root of all evil (1 Tim. 6:10). Note that not money, but the love of money is the cause of further sin. Jesus' warning against Mammon has always played a significant role in Christian ethics. "On the basis of the First Commandment, the antithesis between God and Mammon determined Luther's economic thought."[14] A thorough investigation of Jesus' statements in the Sermon on the Mount demonstrates that they not only censure those who live only for Mammon (or, as Marx would say, for capital). Mammon has been raised to a religion , a rival to Biblical faith in God. Had Jesus not used the name of a heathen deity, we would understand this better. He could have said that we should have only one God. We pray either to the God of the Bible or to Mammon, but, as we know, "Mammon" refers not to a deity, but to wealth, money and capital. In Lk. 16:13, Jesus repeats, "You cannot serve both God and Money (Greek *Mammon*)," but a few verses earlier (Lk. 16:9, 11) he uses the term to describe the money used in business. The religion of Mammon can thus replace faith in the God of the Bible. This was the factor that prevented the rich young ruler from following Jesus, for he loved his wealth more than God (Mt. 19:16-30; Mk. 10:17-31; Lk. 18:18-30). The young man had kept all the commandments except the first, "You shall have no other gods before me." Even though the religion of money has no gods, no priests, no temple (none that we would call temples), it is an atheistic religion, one without God (Greek *a*=without; *theos*=God). Is Jesus comparing two things that are not comparable? Isn't God a religious issue and "Mammon" a matter of economics, business and lifestyle?

---

serve as 'opium for the people' to prevent them from criticising the powers that be. I know of no other holy scripture in any other religion that so harshly criticises rulers who gain wealth by unjust means and violence. In fact, Scripture condemns the unjust believer most of all. To be sure, many Christian bishops and church leaders have been guilty, but the Bible's social criticism is often directed against the religious leadership who oppress their own people and disregard the basis of their religion.

[14] Hans-Jürgen Prien. *Luthers Wirtschaftsethik*. Vandenhoeck & Ruprecht: Göttingen, 1992, p. 221 (See the whole book on the significance of the Sermon on the Mount for Luther's economic ethics). See also the numerous references to Mammon in Luther's writings. *Martin Luthers Sämtliche Schriften*, ed. by Joh. Georg Walch. Vol. 23. Verlag der Lutherischen Buchhandlung H. Harms: Groß Oesingen, 1986 (Reprint from 1910²), Col 1130-1132.

Religion is never a theoretical matter in the Bible. The question is not whether a movement, a philosophy, or a lifestyle considers itself a religion or not, but whether it is ultimately that which determines the values of our everyday lives in reality, not merely in theory. Above all, Scripture is concerned with hope and faith in the God of the Bible. The question is not whether we are convinced that God exists, but whether we hope existentially in Him. "You believe that there is one God. Good! Even the demons believe that — and shudder" (Jas. 2:19). In both the Old Testament and the New, the word translated "believe" means "to trust, to depend on, to consider reliable," which obviously includes hope. If we believe in God, we consider Him absolutely reliable, take seriously all that He has said and done as Creator and Saviour, and plan our lives according to His existence and His Law.

Religion is anything that competes with this Biblical hope and this faith. What do I rely on completely? What gives my life its fundamental meaning? What controls my heart? What determines my decisions? Who has the last word in my life? What is my final goal? What do I love most? How do I justify my desires?

Job once acknowledged God's right to judge him "if I have put my trust in gold or said to pure gold, 'You are my security'" (Job 31:24). Although 'hope' and 'trust' are words that can only apply to God, we often use them to refer to disguised religions, as Job's admission shows. Proverbs repeat this idea: "Whoever trusts in his riches will fall" (Pr. 11:28). We could also say, "Whoever trusts in wealth." Psalm 49:6 speaks of "those who trust in their wealth and boast of their great riches" (See also Ps. 52:7). The Bible frequently describes the religion of money with the same terms it uses to describe man's relationship to God.

In 1 Timothy 6:17, Paul exhorts the rich not to set their hope on wealth, "which is so uncertain," but in God. In Ephesians 5:3-5, he warns against greed, and in agreement with the Old Testament, adds, "for it is idolatry."

16. The Battle Against Pseudo-Hopes

Proposition: God will disappoint false hopes and wants us to expose them prophetically.

Speaking to God, Job says, "You destroy man's hope" (Job 14:19). Even believers are sometimes led by God into absolutely hopeless situations, so that they learn to surrender any hopes except God Himself. Jeremiah, author of Lamentations, cries out, "Why have you afflicted us so that we cannot be healed? We hoped for peace but no good has come, for a time of healing but there is only terror" (Jer. 14:19; see also 8:15).

For this reason, one of the Old Testament prophets' most important responsibilities was to repudiate pseudo-hopes, whether in the form of false gods, deceptive political alliances, deceitful promises of kings, or the optimistic predictions of lying prophets. We must not depend on men (Jer. 17:5; 48:13), on our own righteousness (Ezek. 33:13), on religious symbols such as the Temple (Jer. 7:4), or on idols (Hab. 2:18), but only on God.

Europe's history has been shaped by false prophets like Hitler and Stalin, and by many other less-known deceivers. The prophetic unmasking of such deceptive hopes is one of the most important responsibilities of European churches and believers; a responsibility in which we have failed much too often.

God Gives Hope

17. God Himself has always been the Giver of Hope – from the very beginning of history

Proposition: World hope begins with the fact that God is the first missionary.

God has always been the first missionary. Immediately after the Fall, man's history seemed to have ended before it had really begun, but God did not give up. In grace, He visited the Garden of Eden (Gen. 3:8-9), seeking for Adam and Eve, and calling, "Where are you?" (Gen. 3:9). In proclaiming both future judgment and future redemption (Gen. 3:14-21), He Himself gave new hope to Creation.

18. God Himself Brings Hope – in Jesus

Proposition: Jesus is the prototype of the missionary and the bringer of hope.

Jesus was sent to earth by God. As a human being, He was to bear our punishment on the Cross in order to effect and proclaim our salvation and thus to restore hope and a future for the world. Even before Creation God had purposed (Eph. 1:4) not to leave us up to the fate of sin, which we had brought upon ourselves, but to send Himself in Christ as a missionary to the world in order to make a true future possible (Jn. 3:16).

19. God Himself Gives Us Hope – in the Holy Spirit

Proposition: Pentecost shows us that world mission in the power of the Holy Spirit is the most important mark of the New Testament Church, and that Christians could neither hope nor proclaim hope without Him.

Jesus often charged the disciples to wait for the coming of the Holy Spirit before they began to evangelise the nations (Mk. 16:15-20; Acts 1:4-11). The Spirit was to come as Jesus' successor in order to convince the world of the Gospel (Jn. 16:7-11). With His coming upon His Church, both the New Testament Church and world mission began. Without Him no form of missions or missionary strategy would have any prospects of success, for only He can convict of sin (Jn. 16:7-10), lead to acknowledgement of God and of the saving work of Jesus Christ, regenerate sinners, or give them hope (Jn. 3:5). Certainly God has chosen to use human beings in missions and intends for them to use their minds in order to reach others,[15] but all such strategies are only provisory, since God alone decides whether or not they are successful (1 Cor. 12:4-6; Rom. 1:13).

Paul, in particular, continually emphasises that it is the Holy Spirit who pours hope into our hearts and that our hope is completely dependent on His unbelievable power. Let me give you three examples. "And hope does not disappoint us, because God has poured out his love into our hearts by the Holy Spirit, whom he has given us" (Rom. 5:5). "May the God of hope fill you with all joy and peace as you trust in him, so that you may overflow with hope by the power of the Holy Spirit" (Rom. 15:13). "But by faith we eagerly await through the Spirit the righteousness for which we hope" (Gal. 5:5).

20. God Himself Gives Us Hope – in the Church, the Bearer of Hope

Proposition: The Church's mission is based on the fact that God first sent Himself into the world as a missionary (*Missio Dei*).

---

[15] Paul, for example, made many detailed plans and developed a general strategy. See Romans 1 and 15, for example.

Jesus sent His disciples into the world to carry out the commission which He had received from His Father (Mt. 10:40; Mk. 9:37; Lk. 10:16; Acts 3:20, 26; and about 50 times in John, beginning with Jn. 3:17; see also Isa. 48:16), and which the Holy Spirit had received from the Father and the Son (Jn. 14:26; 15:26; Lk. 24:49). In John 17:18 Jesus addresses His Father: "As you sent me into the world, I have sent them into the world." In John 20:21 He converts the statement into a personal address to the disciples: "Again Jesus said, 'Peace be with you! As the Father has sent me, I am sending you'" (Jn. 20:21). God the Father sends His Son and His Spirit as the first missionaries; the Church continues to carry out their mission through world missions. Christian missionary endeavour is thus grounded in the Triune God. Christ's Church is per definition the bearer of hope, for her proclamation of hope in the Gospel is the direct continuation of God's commission.

21. Christ in Us, the Hope of Glory

Proposition: Since God is our only hope, Christ and His saving work on the Cross are our only hope.

When thinking of the Thessalonians, Paul remembers "before our God and Father your work produced by faith, your labour prompted by love, and your endurance inspired by hope in our Lord Jesus Christ" (1 Thes. 1:3).

Christians are of "Christ Jesus our hope" (1 Tim. 1:1), and Christ is in us, for Paul writes, "To them God has chosen to make known among the Gentiles the glorious riches of this mystery, which is Christ in you, the hope of glory" (Col. 1:27).

Hope in Christ is not only in us; we await its concrete, historical and personal fulfilment "while we wait for the blessed hope – the glorious appearing of our great God and Saviour, Jesus Christ" (Tit. 2:13).

22. Hope Through the Cross

Proposition: God's most wonderful act, the basis of all true hope, was the death of Christ on the Cross of Golgotha, where he died on our behalf in order to defeat death, sin and the Devil, the mortal enemies of all hope. For this reason, there can be no hope for a new beginning without forgiveness.

The universal truth that hope for the future depends on forgiveness is just as true in specific cases. Only in forgiving each other can we hope for a new beginning.

Islam, for example, has no doctrines of original sin or of sin as the destruction of man's relationship to God, of reconciliation or forgiveness. For Muslims, reconciliation in private life or between nations is hard to achieve, for past wrongs can still be dug up centuries later.

Whether they personally believed in a reconciliatory God or not, Konrad Adenauer and Charles de Gaulle, as representatives of their nations, acted in the spirit of a civilisation deeply influenced by the Christian faith, when they reconciled Germany and France and decided to begin a new relationship in spite of the terrible injustices of the past. Islam has nothing comparable.

Europe's churches and their believers must forgive each other and be reconciled, if Europe is to find new hope. European families must forgive each other and be reconciled, if Europe is to find new hope. Europe's 'races' and nations must forgive each other and be reconciled, if Europe is to find new hope and a good future. Above all, we must practice forgiveness toward Muslims. Some may have lived here all their lives and some have come recently, but their faith and their culture know nothing of forgiveness, of forgetting past injuries in order to come to terms with the present. Our testimony has no value to them as long as we do not practice forgiveness, and show them that forgiveness means leaving mistakes and sins of the past up to God. Do Christian marriages have hope based on forgiveness and reconciliation? Can a spirit of reconciliation and forgiveness be felt in our churches, so that we have authority and influence, or are we just as driven by tension, rumours, ancient feuds, mobbing and skirmishing, as other organisations are?

23. Hope of Christ's Second Coming and the Resurrection of the Dead

Proposition: Christian hope is directed toward the Second Coming of Christ and the Resurrection of the Dead. Not by chance, the Apostles' Creed ends with lavish descriptions of the future. The Christian faith is not just belief in an omnipotent Creator, but also faith in His saving activity in human history, past and future.

The Future in the Apostles' Creed
(printed in italics)
I believe in one God
the Father Almighty,
Maker of Heaven and earth,

and in Jesus Christ
His only son our Lord;
who was conceived by the Holy Spirit,
born of the virgin Mary
suffered under Pontius Pilate
crucified, dead and buried
he descended into Hell,
the third day he rose from the dead;
he ascended into heaven;
and sitteth at the right hand of God
the Father Almighty;
from thence he shall come
to judge the quick and the dead.
I believe in the Holy Ghost;
the holy catholic Church;
the communion of saints
the forgiveness of sins;
the resurrection of the body
and the life everlasting. Amen.

From the standpoint of this great future, our present little future increases in its significance.

Paul and the Hope of Resurrection

Acts 24:15 "And I have the same hope in God as these men, that there will be a resurrection of both the righteous and the wicked."

Acts 26:6 "And now it is because of my hope in what God has promised our fathers that I am on trial today."

Acts 26:7 "This is the promise our twelve tribes are hoping to see fulfilled as they earnestly serve God day and night. O king, it is because of this hope that the Jews are accusing me."

Acts 28:20 "For this reason I have asked to see you and talk with you. It is because of the hope of Israel that I am bound with this chain."

1 Thes. 4:13 "Brothers, we do not want you to be ignorant about those who fall asleep, or to grieve like the rest of men, who have no hope."

God Is Trustworthy

24. Our Hope in God Is Sure, Because God Is Trustworthy

Proposition: Only hope in God is truly sure, because only God is eternal, unchanging, omnipotent, righteous, wise and loving.

As the Church Father Chrysostom once said, the Christian faith is completely assured, for its founder lives in eternity.[16] Jeremiah based his hope on God's Creatorship: "Do any of the worthless idols of the nations bring rain? Do the skies themselves send down showers? No, it is you, O LORD our God. Therefore our hope is in you, for you are the one who does all this" (Jer. 14: 22).

25. Hope Is Sure Because of God's Faithfulness and His Promise

Proposition: Hope is sure, because it is founded on God's promises, which are reliable, because God Himself has bound Himself to keep them.

Martin Luther wrote, "God's mercy, which promises out of Grace, and Truth, which fulfils the promises, are the causes of hope."

In secular Greek, the word family for 'hope' includes all sorts of expectations, such as dread, fear, hope, wish and want. (For example, 'I hope that the weather will be good tomorrow!') The words have the same everyday meaning in some scriptures; for example, when Paul plans to visit certain churches (for example, Rom. 15:24; 1 Cor. 16:7; Phil. 2:23; 1 Tim. 3:14).

Faith's hope is no vague feeling about the future, however. It is a conviction based on God's absolutely reliable faithfulness. "Let us hold unswervingly to the hope we profess, for he who promised is faithful" (Heb. 10:23). In contrast to the German proverb, "Hoping and waiting make fools of the patient,"[17] Paul tells us, "And hope does not disappoint us" (Rom. 5:5). "Then you will know that I am the LORD; those who hope in me will not be disappointed" (Isa. 49:23).

---

[16] 9. Homilie, Ch. 5.

[17] 'Hoffen und Harren hält manchen zum Narren'.

It is neither conceivable nor possible for God to lie. Our faith and knowledge rest "on the hope of eternal life, which God, who does not lie, promised before the beginning of time" (Tit. 1:2).

26. Our Hope Is Founded on God's Oath

Proposition: We can only rely fully on God, because He has bound Himself by oath to His Covenant.

Unlike the God of Islam, God has sworn: "God did this so that, by two unchangeable things in which it is impossible for God to lie, we who have fled to take hold of the hope offered to us may be greatly encouraged" (Heb. 6:18).

Some say that swearing is necessary only when one wants to avoid telling the truth! But if we insist that it is unnecessary to swear, since we are always to tell the truth, we must explain why God, Who never lies, often swears oaths (for example, Gen. 22:16; Mic. 7:20; Ex. 6:8; Ezek. 20:5; Ps. 95:11). Georg Giesen[18] has counted eighty-two oaths made by God in the Old Testament, 38 percent of all the oaths mentioned. Besides these, God made numerous oaths designated by other terms. God keeps His own commandment that all oaths must be sworn in His name, for "When God made his promise to Abraham, since there was no one greater for him to swear by, he swore by himself" (Heb. 6:13).

God Swears By Himself

Gen. 22:16 "'I swear by myself,' declares the LORD, 'that because you have done this and have not withheld your son, your only son … .'"

Heb. 6:13 "When God made his promise to Abraham, since there was no one greater for him to swear by, he swore by himself."

Jer. 44:26 "But hear the word of the LORD, all Jews living in Egypt: 'I swear by my great name,' says the LORD, 'that no one from Judah living anywhere in Egypt will ever again invoke my name or swear, "As surely as the Sovereign LORD lives."'"

---

[18] Georg Giesen. *Die Wurzel sb' "schwören": Eine semasiologische Studie zum Eid im Alten Testament.* Bonner Biblische Beiträge 56. Peter Hanstein: Königstein, 1981.

Amos 6:8 "The Sovereign LORD has sworn by himself – the LORD God Almighty declares: 'I abhor the pride of Jacob and detest his fortresses; I will deliver up the city and everything in it.'"

Ex. 32:13 "Remember your servants Abraham, Isaac and Israel, to whom you swore by your own self: 'I will make your descendants as numerous as the stars in the sky and I will give your descendants all this land I promised them, and it will be their inheritance forever.'"

Amos 4:2 "The Sovereign LORD has sworn by his holiness: 'The time will surely come when you will be taken away with hooks, the last of you with fishhooks.'"

Deut. 32:40 "I lift my hand to heaven and declare: As surely as I live forever, ..."

1 Sam. 2:30 "Therefore the LORD, the God of Israel, declares: 'I promised that your house and your father's house would minister before me forever.' But now the LORD declares: 'Far be it from me! Those who honour me I will honour, but those who despise me will be disdained.'"

Rom. 14:11 "It is written: 'As surely as I live,' says the Lord, 'every knee will bow before me; every tongue will confess to God.'"

"By myself I have sworn" (Isa. 45:23; Jer. 22:5; 49:13).

"As surely as I live" (Num. 14:21,28; Deut. 32:40; Isa. 49:18; Jer. 22:24; 46:18; Ezek. 5:11; 14: 16,18,20; 16:48; 17:16,19; 18:3; 20:3,31,33; 33:11,27; 34:8; 35:1,6; Zeph. 2:9; Rom. 14:11).

God's oath, in which He binds Himself to His covenant, is essential to the Christian faith. We often fail to recognise this, because we no longer understand the meaning of an oath, or because we are no longer aware of the vital differences between the God of the Bible and the gods of other religions. In Islam God is so absolute, sovereign and independent, that he would never commit himself absolutely to any human being, for that would make him subject to human judgement. Even when he promises, Allah retains the right to change his mind, without anyone being able or competent to condemn Him.

The God of the Judaeo-Christian tradition is equally absolute, sovereign and independent. No one could forbid Him to change His plans or force Him to keep His promises. Neither Mankind nor Creation confine God, but He Himself has bound Himself to His own word and has sworn in His own Name to keep it. God is faithful, and absolutely reliable. In contrast to Allah, His sovereignty expresses itself in the fact that no one can force Him to fulfil His plans, honour His oaths or keep His promises. In fact, He charges us to measure Him according to His own words and to 'take Him to court' (Isa. 1:18; 41:1; 43:26; Mal. 3:10), but man will never find Him at fault.

God's faithfulness leads to trust, or, as we usually express it, to faith, which is one of the three most common descriptions (faith, love and hope; See Proposition 2) of our relationship to God – not by chance.

If God and Jesus Themselves swear more than anyone else, then the purpose of swearing cannot be to distinguish truth from untruth. God swears more than anyone else, and the Bible's great men of faith follow His example. How can the truth of a statement be suspect, when God has spoken?[19] The author of the Epistle to the Hebrews explains God's oath to Abraham with the following words: "Men swear by someone greater than themselves, and the oath confirms what is said and puts an end to all argument. Because God wanted to make the unchanging nature of his purpose very clear to the heirs of what was promised, he confirmed it with an oath. God did this so that, by two unchangeable things in which it is impossible for God to lie, we who have fled to take hold of the hope offered to us may be greatly encouraged." (Heb. 6:16-18) The eternal reliability of God's decision thus lies in His oath, for it makes the covenant final and irrevocable. Not every statement made by God is irrevocable: how often has He repealed the judgement He had proclaimed, because the sinner repented! Judgements were unavoidable only when God had proclaimed them under oath. Human oaths have the same meaning: the difference between a promise and an oath is that a

---

[19] Assuming that Jesus was defending the Old Testament view of swearing against the practice of the scribes and pharisees, who swore by everything except by God, then the Sermon on the Mount does not condemn all oaths, but only those forbidden in the Old Testament. In Matthew 5:34-35, Jesus is saying, "Do not swear at all by Heaven ... or by the earth." James 5:12 expresses the same idea: "swear neither by heaven nor by the earth." Properly translated, the texts should read: "But I say to you: You should not swear at all by heaven, for it is God's throne, nor by the earth, for it is His footstool, nor by Jerusalem, for she is the city of the great King, nor should you swear by your head, for you cannot make a single hair white or black. Let your speech be Yes, yes! or No, no! Anything more is from the Evil One" (Mt. 5:34-37).

promise can be revoked under circumstances. An oath makes the difference between flirting and marriage, for marriage is a covenant made by oath.

Let us return to the reliability of divine hope. According to Hebrews 7:20-21, the Old Testament Levitical priesthood was not based on oath, whereas Jesus' eternal priesthood in the order of Melchizedek was based on the oath made by God in Psalm 110:4: "The LORD has sworn and will not change his mind: You are a priest forever, in the order of Melchizedek." Hebrews 7:20-22 tells us, "And it was not without an oath! Others became priests without any oath, but he became a priest with an oath when God said to him: 'The Lord has sworn and will not change his mind: 'You are a priest forever.'" "Because of this oath, Jesus has become the guarantee of a better covenant" (Heb 7:20-22). The Levitical priesthood could end, because God had not assured its eternal existence by oath, but Jesus' priesthood will never cease, for its eternal validity has been sealed with an oath.

27. Hope Implies Activity

Proposition: The security of our hope does not permit us to rest in future dreams, but requires us to endeavour to confirm our faith. "We want each of you to show this same diligence to the very end, in order to make your hope sure" (Heb. 6:11). Paul admonishes the believers to "continue in your faith, established and firm, not moved from the hope held out in the gospel" (Col. 1:23).

28. Hope Is Founded on the Word of God

Proposition: Because God, Who is absolutely faithful, has bound Himself – in writing[20] – His Word is the reliable basis of our hope.

The Psalmist confesses before men, "I wait for the LORD, my soul waits, and in his word I put my hope" (Ps. 130:5), and to God, "May those who fear you

---

[20] Article 1.1. of the Westminster Confession: "… therefore it pleased the Lord, at sundry times, and in divers manners, to reveal himself, and to declare that his will unto his Church; and afterwards, for the better preserving and propagation of the truth and for the more sure establishment and comfort of the Church … to commit the same wholly unto writing." G. I. Williamson. *The Westminster Confession of Faith for Study Classes.* Philadelphia, Pennsylvania: Presbyterian and Reformed Publishing Company, 1964.

rejoice when they see me, for I have put my hope in your word" (Ps. 119:74); "Do not snatch the word of truth from my mouth, for I have put my hope in your laws" (Ps. 119:43); "You are my refuge and my shield; I have put my hope in your word" (Ps. 119:114). After Jesus had achieved eternal life for us, Paul repeats this Old Testament truth in speaking of the faith and truth "that spring from the hope that is stored up for you in heaven and that you have already heard about in the word of truth, the gospel."

Let me repeat: Christians study the Bible in order to find hope for themselves, for their families, for their churches and for their society. "For everything that was written in the past was written to teach us, so that through endurance and the encouragement of the Scriptures we might have hope." (Rom. 15:4)

European Christians must proclaim that churches and believers who reject God's Word as unreliable or irrelevant rob not only themselves but all Europe of its only truly reliable hope. God does not require us to depend on some nebulous expectation, but has given us concrete promises in His written Word. The deceptive hopes of critical theologians must be exposed in our continent more than anywhere else in the world. Many European churches despair, because they no longer know what they can hope for! Without the Bible, they will never know!

29. Our Hope Is Based on God's Activity – not on Lectures

Proposition: Our hope depends, not on theories or divine intentions, but on God's activity. In the Bible hope and love are never exhausted in words or feelings, but are always expressed in action. Paul speaks of "faith expressing itself through love" (Gal. 5:5-6). 1 John 3:17-18 admonishes, "If anyone has material possessions and sees his brother in need but has no pity on him, how can the love of God be in him? Dear children, let us not love with words or tongue but with actions and in truth."

John bases his commandment in Jesus' ministry: "This is how we know what love is: Jesus Christ laid down his life for us. And we ought to lay down our lives for our brothers" (1 Jn. 3:16). Jesus' love can be seen in his conduct. His death is the proof of God's love (Rom. 5:8; Jn. 3:16; Eph. 5:25). Husbands are to demonstrate their love for their wives in action and self-sacrifice, as Christ demonstrated His love for the church. "Husbands, love your wives, just as Christ loved the church and gave himself up for her" (Eph. 5:25).

In the Book of Revelation, John distinguishes between love and lovelessness not in words but in conduct. "Yet I hold this against you: You have forsaken your first love. ... Repent and do the things you did at first. ... I know your deeds, your love and faith, your service and perseverance, and that you are now doing more than you did at first" (Rev. 2:4-5, 19). To return to the first love means to act as one had in the beginning. The first love was not exhausted in feelings, but expressed itself in action. As the Manila Manifesto of the Lausanne Movement reminds us, the unchanging Gospel must become visible in the changed lives of believers. The proclamation of God's love must be accompanied by loving service. Preaching the Gospel of the Kingdom of God implies commitment to His expectations of justice and peace."[21]

Europe will not return to her first love or her hope until Christians proclaim God's Word and act accordingly.

Hope Changes Our Conduct

30. True Hope Assumes that God Is Omnipotent

Proposition: We have no true reason to hope, unless we believe and know that God has everything under control. True hope is based on the profession: "I believe in one God, the Father Almighty, Maker of Heaven and earth."

God Is Omnipotent

Job 42:2 "I know that you can do all things; no plan of yours can be thwarted."

Jer. 32:17: "Ah, Sovereign LORD, you have made the heavens and the earth by your great power and outstretched arm. Nothing is too hard for you."

Gen. 18:14: "Is anything too hard for the LORD?"

Mt. 28:18: "All authority in heaven and on earth has been given to me."

---

[21] *Das Manifest von Manila.* Lausanner Bewegung – Deutscher Zweig: Stuttgart, 1996. p. 14.

Isa 55:11: "So is my word that goes out from my mouth: It will not return to me empty, but will accomplish what I desire and achieve the purpose for which I sent it."

Job 36:22-23: "God is exalted in his power. Who is a teacher like him? Who has prescribed his ways for him, or said to him, 'You have done wrong'?"

2 Chr. 14:11: "LORD, there is no one like you to help the powerless against the mighty. Help us, O LORD our God, for we rely on you."

Ps. 33:10-11: "The LORD foils the plans of the nations; he thwarts the purposes of the peoples. But the plans of the LORD stand firm forever."

God called "Omnipotent": Gen. 17:1; 28:3; 43:14; 48:3; 49:25; Ex. 6:3; Num. 24:4; Ruth 1:20-21; Job 40:2 (30 times in the Book of Job); Ps. 68:15; Ps. 91:1; Isa. 13:6; Ezek. 1:24; Rev. 1:8; 4:8; 11:17; 15:3; 16:7,14; 19:6,15; 21:22

Only when we believe this, can we assume that God will bring all to a good end. One example from the New Testament and one from the Old will have to suffice. David proclaims: "Commit your way to the LORD; trust in him and he will do this" (Ps. 37:5). Paul rejoices, "And we know that in all things God works for the good of those who love him, who have been called according to his purpose. ... For I am convinced that neither death nor life, neither angels nor demons, neither the present nor the future, nor any powers, neither height nor depth, nor anything else in all creation, will be able to separate us from the love of God that is in Christ Jesus our Lord" (Rom. 8:28, 38-39).

31. Hope Gives Us Security and Peace of Mind

Proposition: Hope gives us peace of mind, even though our own problems and worldwide suffering could drive us mad. "You will be secure, because there is hope; you will look about you and take your rest in safety" (Job 11:18). The psalmist prayed, "Find rest, O my soul, in God alone; my hope comes from him" (Ps. 62:5). The Church Father Chrysostom described hope as a strong cord that hangs down from Heaven and holds our souls.[22]

No human being can bear all the problems of the world, not even all the problems in his own life. One day's problems suffice (Mt. 6:34). Anyone who studies the world as seriously as the author of Ecclesiastes (see Proposition

---

[22] *To Theodore,* Ch. 2.

56) could lose his mind at the thought of all the injustice, meaninglessness, suffering and destruction of our world, but anyone who places his trust in the One Who has "got the whole world in His hands," as the American slaves once sang, can still continue to live courageously.

32. Hope Gives Courage

Proposition: Christian hope gives us the courage to act, "Therefore, since we have such a hope, we are very bold" (2 Cor. 3:12). Courage and boldness are closely related to hope (Heb. 3:6). Hope and trust drive out fear (Isa. 12:2; Ps. 46:3; Prov. 28:1), even the fear of failure.

European Christians must learn that we will need hope in the future in the face of increasing persecution and minority status, even in countries with an ancient Christian tradition and religious freedom. We need courage to face both believers and hypocrites, who conform in form only.

33. Hope Makes us both Optimistic and Realistic –
Giving-up is not an Option

Proposition: Once we learn to distinguish between deceptive hopes and true hope, we can be both optimistic and realistic. Peter wrote, "be self-controlled; set your hope fully on the grace to be given you when Jesus Christ is revealed" (1 Pet. 1:13).

Something of this optimistic realism will become visible to the world. Otherwise Peter would not have to challenge us to justify our hope to those around us (1 Pet. 3:15). The apostles assume that others will notice the hope 'in us'.

Biblical hope resides in the complementarity of pessimistic attitudes toward human nature and an optimistic confidence in God's possibilities, in the tension between the 'already' and the 'not yet', as theologians have formulated it. Neither side of a complementary system can be excluded.

Europe needs optimistic Christians – not dreamers, fanatics, demagogues or unrealistic prophets of doom, but realists who take problems seriously, but because they take God just as seriously and expect His intervention, they radiate hope and optimism. The young generation of European Christians can't afford new pessimistic hindrances; they need courageous, forward-looking role models.

Excursus: On the complementarity of Biblical thinking

Physicists have discovered many phenomena which can only be described as complementary (Lat. *Complementum*: 'Completion'). Some of these phenomena exist in paired complementarities, some in triple complementarities. We speak of complementary colours, such as red and green, which blend to become white. An electron can only be observed as either a particle or as a wave, but not as both within one experiment. The same is true of light.

The theory of complementarity was controversial at first. The Dane Niels Bohr (1885-1962), who received the Nobel Prize in 1922, introduced the concept in 1927[23] and assured the victory of complementary thought in Twentieth-Century physics.[24]

"Complementarity [Lat.], a phenomenon first observed by N. Bohr, recognises that atomic particles have two paired, linked but apparently contradictory characteristics, for example, particle and wave. It is, however, impossible to observe both characteristics simultaneously, for both factors require measuring procedures which disrupt each other."[25]

Complementary thought means that two, three, or more aspects of a phenomenon can only be observed and described independently of each other, although the individual results and statements are equally valid, and although the student can only assure an accurate result when all elements are properly related to each other. Complementary colours, for example, produce white only when they are properly mixed.

Carl Friedrich von Weizsäcker defines complementarity as follows:

"Complementarity consists in the fact that the elements cannot be considered simultaneously although both must be employed."[26]

---

[23] Carl Friedrich von Weizsäcker. "Komplementarität und Logik", pp. 281-331 in: Carl Friedrich von Weizsäcker. *Zum Weltbild der Physik*. S. Hirzel: Stuttgart, 1958[7], p. 281.

[24] See Wolfgang Buchheim. Komplementarität nach Niels Bohr. Sitzungsberichte der Sächsischen Akademie der Wissenschaften zu Leipzig, Mathematisch-Naturwissenschaftliche Klasse 117, 6. Akademie-Verlag: Berlin, 1984 and Wolfgang Buchheim (ed.). Beiträge zur Komplementarität, the same series, 55,5. Ibid. 1983.

[25] *Bertelsmann Neues Lexikon in 10 Vols*. Vol 5. Bertelsmann Lexikon Verlag: Gütersloh, 1995, p. 323.

[26] Carl Friedrich von Weizsäcker. "Komplementarität und Logik". op. cit., p. 284, defining the classical view of complementarity. His own opinion is somewhat different.

In the meantime, this way of thinking has spread from physics to other natural sciences and areas of life.[27]

This view is not illogical: human limitations make us dependent on complementary explanations of Biblical truth. The Early Church intentionally formulated the most central dogmas of the Christian faith in complementary form, as it defended the truths that God is triune or that Jesus is simultaneously very God and very Man.

The complementary nature of Biblical truth can play an important role in overcoming unnecessary disputes between Christians.[28] We tend to emphasise one side of a complementary truth at the expense of the other, just as some theologians used to emphasise Jesus' human nature in order to disprove His divine nature, or to point to His obedience in order to refute the doctrine of His equality to the Father in Being and rank.

Biblical truth includes many complementary doctrines besides the Trinity and the Double Nature of Christ:

- Predestination and responsibility
- Faith and knowledge
- Law and grace
- Condemnation and pardon
- God's love and His wrath
- Doctrine and life
- Baptism as an act of God and an act of man
- the necessity of church office and the universal priesthood of believers[29]
- or the differences and equality of Man and Woman.[30]

---

[27] See, for example, Helmut K. Reich. *Der Begriff der Komplementarität in Wissenschaft und Alltag.* Berichte zur Erziehungswissenschaft 105. Pädagogisches Institut Freiburg (CH), 1994.

[28] See Winfried Amelung. *In IHM ist die Fülle: Wider die falschen Alternativen.* Weinmann-Stiftung: Dornstetten, 1988.

[29] Ibid., pp. 33-50 (Church office) und pp. 51-69 (baptism).

[30] See John Stott. Christsein in den Brennpunkten unserer Zeit ... 4 ... im sexuellen Bereich. Francke: Marburg, 1988 [Engl. 1984]. pp. 21-24 (Abschnitt "Komplementarität").

Scripture introduces all of these topics with two or more seemingly contradictory aspects, which, however, cannot be disassociated from each other, but can only be contemplated one at a time.

34. If We Expect What Is Humanly Impossible, We Will Do All That Is Humanly Possible

Proposition: When we rely on what is humanly impossible, we will do all we can to achieve it, for hope makes us active! "Trust in the LORD and do good" (Ps. 37:3). It is hopelessness that makes us passive, weak and timid.

35. Hope Makes Us Calm, but Not Lazy and Inactive

Proposition: "To hope is to be moved forward toward the goal,"[31] for hope is the historical dynamic of faith.

Oskar Cullmann writes, "True Christian eschatology never nourishes passivity, inactivity or immobility."[32] If hope leads to a calmness characterised by inactivity and laziness, why does the Bible remind us so often that hope gives strength (Isa. 40:31; 30:15) and can only come from the power of the Holy Spirit (Rom. 15:13)?

No, hope gives us a serenity which is sober and active. Hope stimulates no frenzied activism, but a rational activity for others' sake. Action is part of hope: "Maintain love and justice, and wait for your God always" (Hos. 12:7), for "The desire of the righteous ends only in good, but the hope of the wicked only in wrath" (Prov. 11:23).

Only because so many Christians in earlier generations were motivated by hope, did Europe ever become a Christian continent. We will not regain Europe for Jesus, unless we expect everything from God and begin to act!

36. Hope Makes Us Active and Assertive

Proposition: Hope makes us willing to act, to take risks instead of just talking! "And for this we labour and strive, that we have put our hope in the liv-

---

[31] Ernst G. Hoffmann in *Theologisches Wörterbuch zum Neuen Testament*, II, 726.

[32] Oskar Cullmann. *Jesus und die Revolutionäre seiner Zeit*. Mohr Siebeck: Tübingen, 1970, p. 29.

ing God, who is the Saviour of all men, and especially of those who believe" (1 Tim. 4:10).

Too many European Christians have sat around too long, when our hope should have driven us to action. Only when we seek to help others, even when all is against us, will our hope become real for others.

37. Hope Gives Us New Priorities, Which Enable Us to Forego Privileges

Proposition: Hope changes our priorities, which are then expressed in the willingness to do without, to sacrifice, and to accept disadvantages. Those who compete, are willing to sacrifice comfort in order to win. (1 Cor. 9:25).

Peter, speaking of women, shows that we can forego things important to others (here, clothing and jewelry), because our hope has changed our values. The "holy women of the past who put their hope in God" made themselves beautiful with inner values (1 Pet. 3:5). When we hold fast to our values under pressure, we experience the strength that our hope give us, for "suffering produces perseverance; perseverance, character; and character, hope" (Rom. 5:3-4).

Every kind of hope for the future influences our present activity. Christians are no exception: our hope for the reality that God has promised should change us for the better. "Everyone who has this hope in him purifies himself, just as he is pure" (1 Jn. 3:3).

38. Hope Makes Us Understanding and Patient with Others

Proposition: Patience is a high Christian virtue which grows out of hope. When we have hope for others, we will also be more understanding. "But if we hope for what we do not yet have, we wait for it patiently" (Rom. 8:25). This patience influences our relationship with others (Gal. 5:22; Eph. 4:2; Col. 3:12-13; 1 Tim. 6:11; 2 Tim. 3:10). Paul tells us that love "always protects, always trusts, always hopes, always perseveres" (1 Cor. 13:7).

39. Hope Creates Endurance

Proposition: Hope helps us to endure, when we would prefer to give up. "But those who hope in the LORD will renew their strength. They will soar on wings like eagles; they will run and not grow weary, they will walk and not be faint" (Isa. 40:31). This is true for our personal lives, as well as for the Church and for society.

If we expect the fulfilment of our hopes in the 'distant future', we will be able to wait. The world will notice this attitude here and now.

Many European Christians complain that certain areas of social life once dominated by Christian values are now often dominated by other values. In complaining we ignore the fact that Christian influence has always depended on the long-term endeavours of believers who often never experienced the realisation of their dreams. When we work on legal reform, build colleges, or work with young people without a job, we influence the distant future, and we may not see harvest for many years. We need long-term Christian projects and initiatives in all aspects of creation and church life.

40. Because Hope Anticipates, It Rejoices

Proposition: As long as we have hope, we have reason to rejoice. In spite of serious problems the prophet Isaiah wrote, "In that day they will say, 'Surely this is our God; we trusted in him, and he saved us. This is the LORD, we trusted in him; let us rejoice and be glad in his salvation'" (Isa. 25:9).

And our joy should be full of hope. "Be joyful in hope, patient in affliction, faithful in prayer" (Rom. 12:12).

For this reason, Scripture often speaks of joy and hope at one time. Paul writes, "May the God of hope fill you with all joy and peace as you trust in him, so that you may overflow with hope by the power of the Holy Spirit" (Rom. 15:13; see also 1 Thes. 2:19) and in Proverbs 10:28 we see that "The prospect of the righteous is joy, but the hopes of the wicked come to nothing."

Where there is hope, there is joy. Where the greatest hope is to be found – in the Christian faith – there should be the greatest joy. Unfortunately, this is news to many Europeans, whose practical experience with Christians and with churches speaks a different language. We must learn to rejoice, to celebrate our joy as in the Bible, and to employ the arts, such as music and painting, according to God's will.

Hope in Suffering and Resistance

41. Hope Requires Suffering and Endeavour –
the Awareness of Hopelessness and of Comfort

Proposition: Even those who believe in God can feel hopeless.

The Bible speaks of this situation very honestly. Psalms of lamentation, the book of Job (particularly Job 17:13-15), and Jeremiah's Lamentations honestly portray despair and the feeling of being abandoned by God, without denying them in pious avowals, such as those made by Job's friends. Deep depression can cause us to lose even our hope in God. "So I say, 'My splendour is gone and all that I had hoped from the LORD'" (Lam. 3:18).

In this situation, it is better not to ignore pain, but to endure it with the help of God and friends, and to wait on the Lord. "It is good to wait quietly for the salvation of the LORD" (Lam. 3:26); "But as for me, I watch in hope for the LORD, I wait for God my Saviour; my God will hear me" (Mic. 7:7). Sometimes one may be torn between hope and suspicion of that hope, as Abraham was: "Against all hope, Abraham in hope believed" (Rom. 4:18). Then we can only pray, "I do believe; help me overcome my unbelief!" (Mk. 9:24)

For this reason, we will never learn true hope as long as all goes well, but in difficulties, suffering, illness and sin, even in death. Paul writes, "I eagerly expect and hope that I will in no way be ashamed, but will have sufficient courage so that now as always Christ will be exalted in my body, whether by life or by death" (Phil. 1:20).

Those who have seldom experienced personal suffering can learn the meaning of hope by bearing others' burdens, by sympathising (Heb. 4:15 ; Gr. *sumpatheo* literally means 'to suffer with'). For, as Paul writes, "If one part suffers, every part suffers with it; if one part is honoured, every part rejoices with it" (1 Cor. 12:26).

When the Bible tells us that those who place their hope in God are blessed, it often speaks of people who have experienced intense suffering and despair (for example, Ps. 146:5; 84:12; Jer. 17:7). Christ has not promised us success in this life, and our hope is not restricted to those who are successful. Depression and despair must be endured and that can take time, but in the end, God's hope triumphs. "God did this so that, by two unchangeable things in which it is impossible for God to lie, we who have fled to take hold of the hope offered to us may be greatly encouraged" (Heb. 6:18, see also Ps. 119:49-50). We can be grateful that our heavenly Father "loved us and by his grace gave us eternal encouragement and good hope" (2 Thes. 2:16). Even in his darkest suffering, Job can cry out, "I know that my Redeemer lives" (Job 19:25). We can all pray, "Why are you downcast, O my soul? Why so disturbed within me? Put your hope in God, for I will yet praise him" (Ps. 42:5; see also 42:11 and 43:5).

42. Prayer Leads to Hope, and Hope Leads to Prayer

Proposition: Because prayer is the expression of our hope in God, in despair and hopelessness it becomes our most important comfort. "Be joyful in hope, patient in affliction, faithful in prayer" (Rom. 12:12).

Many of these propositions demonstrate the close relationship between prayer and hope, particularly since many of the Scriptures quoted come from the Bible's prayerbook, the Psalms, which not only contains numerous admonitions to hope only in God, but also many lamentations, begun in times of despair, suffering and hopelessness, that slowly move from despair to hope.

We need this not only in our private lives, but also in our society, for its fate is our fate. Doesn't God command the Israelites to seek the well-being of Babylon, for even though the city is heathen, its fate is the fate of God's people. "Also, seek the peace and prosperity of the city to which I have carried you into exile. Pray to the LORD for it, because if it prospers, you too will prosper" (Jer. 29:7). In the New Testament, Paul bids the church to pray for the government, "I urge, then, first of all, that requests, prayers, intercession and thanksgiving be made for everyone – for kings and all those in authority, that we may live peaceful and quiet lives in all godliness and holiness. This is good, and pleases God our Saviour" (1 Tim. 2:1-3), for the political policies and the state of society also determines the life of the church.

One of the most hopeful signs for Europe, in my opinion, is the eagerness of European Christians to pray and their participation in all sorts of prayer movements, such as Operation World, the Alliance Week of Prayer, the Worldwide Day of Prayer for Persecuted Christians, and 30 Days of Prayer for the Islamic World. Perhaps this results from the prayers of African, Asian and Latin American Christians for Europe!

43. Suffering for Hope's Sake

Proposition: It is not only important to endeavour to hope in suffering, but it is often necessary also to suffer for the sake of our hope. History shows that nothing can be achieved without the willingness to suffer for hope.

Paul insists to his judges that he is on trial "because of my hope in the resurrection of the dead" (Acts 23:6; see also Acts 26:6-7; 28,20; also texts on the resurrection in Proposition 23).

Instead of comfortably proclaiming our hope from the living room sofa, we need to accept the necessity of disadvantages and of concrete suffering for our hope – not because suffering has any value in itself, but because our world causes us to suffer and because our pain highlights the seriousness of the situation.

44. Hope Is Invincible, because It Comes from Within

Proposition: True hope lives in human hearts and thus cannot be conquered by external powers. "And hope does not disappoint us, because God has poured out his love into our hearts by the Holy Spirit, whom he has given us" (Rom. 5:5).

For this reason, we are to "give the reason for the hope that you have" (1 Pet. 3:15). No wonder so many Scriptures speak of the hope in our hearts (for example, Eph. 1:18). And for this reason, true hope means that the Spirit of God transforms our hearts. "I pray also that the eyes of your heart may be enlightened in order that you may know the hope to which he has called you, the riches of his glorious inheritance in the saints" (Eph. 1:18). And for this reason, the secret of hope is that Christ is living "in us." "To them God has chosen to make known among the Gentiles the glorious riches of this mystery, which is Christ in you, the hope of glory" (Col. 1:27).

In the Bible, the heart is the centre of judgement, thought, will, and attitude, the place where we make decisions. The heart governs our lives. When God and His Word control a person's heart, he 'believes in his heart' in the biblical sense of the word (See Mk. 11:23; Rom. 10:9-10; Acts 8:37) and loves God with 'all his heart' (Deut. 6:6; Mt 22:37). Faith and life are one. Speaking of Mammon, Jesus uses the word *heart* in this sense when He says, "For where your treasure is, there your heart will be also" (Mt. 6:21; Lk. 12:34).

45. Hope Is Invincible, because It Comes from Heaven

Proposition: Hope in Eternity gives us strength in space and time. Paul speaks of the "hope that is stored up for you in heaven" (Col. 1:5).

Unbelievers cannot experience true Christian hope, and difficult situations ('the World') cannot overcome it, because it lives within us and because it comes from Heaven.

46. Hope Defends Us Against the Evil One

Proposition: Christian hope protects us against the assaults of evil, for we wear "faith and love as a breastplate, and the hope of salvation as a helmet" (1 Thes. 5:8; see also Eph. 6:17). The most important part of our body, the head, wears hope like a helmet. When we lose that protection, we lose our heads and ourselves as well.

As the Church Father Chrysostom wrote, "Just as the helmet protects our most honourable part, our head, by covering it on all sides, so hope keeps our courage from sinking, and holds it erect, obstructing anything that might fall on it from outside."[33]

Hope protects us, of course, only because God is our guard and because we can rely on Him and on His Word. "You are my refuge and my shield; I have put my hope in your word" (Ps. 119:114).

Hope in the Face of Doomsday Speculation

47. Scripture Justifies the Church's Hope of Growth

Proposition: The success of world missions is guaranteed by the invisible but universal dominion of Jesus Christ.

The success of world missions confirms the promise of Christ's dominion. In the Great Commission in Matthew 28:18-20, He asserts the triumph of world evangelisation with the assurance that "All authority in heaven and on earth has been given to me" (vs. 18) and that "surely I am with you always,

---

[33] 9. Homily, Ch. 5, 8.

to the very end of the age" (vs. 20) – and that in the face of the disciples' doubts (vs. 17). The Great Commission is a promise as well as a commandment, for the Lord will Himself make disciples of all peoples: "I will build my church, and the gates of Hades will not prove stronger than it" (Mt. 16:18). Doesn't the Book of Revelation continually proclaim that people of all languages and cultures will belong to the unnumbered congregation of the redeemed? "And they sang a new song: 'You are worthy to take the scroll and to open its seals, because you were slain, and with your blood you purchased men for God from every tribe and language and people and nation'" (Rev. 5:9-10. See also 7:9; 10:11; 11:9; 13:7; 14:6; 17:15).

Growth is characteristic of the kingdom of God, as the Book of Daniel demonstrates in its many prophetic images, and as Jesus' parables portray the future. Nebuchadnezzar's dream ends with a stone which falls from heaven to destroy the statue of the world kingdoms (Dan. 2:34-35), and then grows in to a great mountain "and filled the whole earth" (Dan. 2:35, 45). Daniel comments, "In the time of those kings, the God of heaven will set up a kingdom that will never be destroyed, nor will it be left to another people. It will crush all those kingdoms and bring them to an end, but it will itself endure forever" (Dan. 2:44). Daniel portrays the end of the world kingdoms symbolised by beasts in the same way (Dan. 7:9-14, 26-27). These kingdoms come to an end when the 'son of man' (Dan. 7:13; Jesus frequently uses the term to refer to Himself) ascends to Heaven (i.e., the Ascension) and receives "authority, glory and sovereign power," so that "all peoples, nations and men of every language worshiped him" (Dan 7:14). This kingdom will not be destroyed (Dan. 7:14, 27). Jesus indeed first established His kingdom at the time of the Roman Empire, beginning with the disciples and the early church, and prophesied in many parables that it would grow until it filled the earth (for example, the parable of the wheat and the tares in Mt. 13:24-30, 36-43; the parable of the mustard seed in Mt. 13:31-32; and the parable of the leaven in Mt. 13:33-35).

Throughout the whole Bible, this promise of growth refers to all aspects of the church, internal and external, spiritual and material, each considered individually or all taken together. This inward and outward growth of the kingdom of God and the church of Jesus Christ does not imply that each and every Christian church, denomination or group will automatically grow – God may discipline His church or permit apostate congregations to die out (See Rev. 2:5; Rom. 11:20-21).

The assurance of the growth and final success of the kingdom of God does not eliminate the possibility of suffering. Particularly parables about growth, such as the parable of the wheat and the tares (Mt. 13:24-30; 36-43), demonstrate clearly that evil matures along with the kingdom. The weeds can endure, however, only because God is letting His church grow and mature. If Christ's church were removed from the earth, final judgment would descend immediately (See Gen. 18:22-23).

48. Hope in the Face of Religious and State Opposition

Proposition: The Revelation of St. John delivers a powerful message which has continually encouraged Christians in history. We should agree on this point, however we may interpret the details of Revelation. The church does not expand through power, wealth or force, but only by Christ's authority, the Word of God and prayer. Even when God permits the powers of religions and states to combine forces against the church, and even when the church seems to be lost, the false church and the perverted state are only digging their own graves when they oppose the church of Jesus. God even leads the powers of the world to fight with each other, so that the political powers destroy the religious opponents of the church, just as the beast of Revelation suddenly turns on the whore of Babylon.

God's kingdom continues to grow in spite of all the religious, intellectual, economic and political powers of this world. Wasn't this spiritual principle obvious in the Old Testament? Didn't Jesus proclaim it in the Great Commission and in the promise that the very gates of Hell could not hinder the kingdom of God?

Hasn't this principle been repeatedly verified in the history of the church? Where is the Roman Empire, where is Manichaism, where are the widespread religions of antiquity who all hated Christianity, but now interest only historians? What happened to National Socialism or to the Communist World Revolution which began in Germany and Russia? Can we not learn from Revelation that the days of Islam, Esoterics and Materialism are also numbered, even if we have no idea when God's wise plan will be revealed?

49. We Still Have Hope, Even in the Face of Impending Judgement

Proposition: Even when God has pronounced judgment, especially when He has pronounced judgment, we can hope.

Jonah was so sure that Nineveh was lost. God's pronouncement sounded as if God's decision was irrevocable: "Forty more days and Nineveh will be overturned" (Jonah 3:4), but there was an unspoken condition, which explains why Jonah had been sent to preach in the first place – "unless you repent and believe!" The city's inhabitants heeded the warning, repented and glorified God, Who then had mercy in spite of His threat (Jonah 3:5-10).

In spite of his anger, Jonah knew that God often acts in this way: "I knew that you are a gracious and compassionate God" (Jonah 4:2). Jonah's complaints and despair were even pious and theologically based! He was "greatly displeased" (Jonah 4:1) that God chose to forgive the Assyrians, although, as a good theologian, he should have realised that God also has mercy on the heathen, "That is why I was so quick to flee" (Jonah 4:2). God provided Jonah with a vine, in order to ease his discomfort, and when He let it wither, Jonah was miserable and wanted to die. Now God could show him how He felt about the lost in Nineveh (Jonah 4:7-11).

Referring to the book of Jonah in his 'Homily on Repentance', the Church Father Chrysostom emphasised that Christian preaching often seems to destroy hope, not in order to crush it, but only to point to the true hope only to be found in God.

God's unimaginable grace expresses itself in the fact that divine pronouncements of judgment are seldom confirmed by oath, which makes them irrevocable, but declarations of grace all the more. The covenant with Noah, that He would never again judge the world in the same way (Gen. 8:20-9:17), was confirmed by oath. In the history of Israel He does the same as Isaiah 54:9 declares: "To me this is like the days of Noah, when I swore that the waters of Noah would never again cover the earth. So now I have sworn not to be angry with you, never to rebuke you again."

50. In the Face of Impending Judgement, God Tests Our   Faith

Proposition: The church preaches judgment only because we have hope. The threat of judgment provides us with unique opportunities to demonstrate our hope in prayer, words and deeds.

Job used the example of a tree that seems to be dead and bare, an image frequently used by Old Testament prophets: "At least there is hope for a tree: If it is cut down, it will sprout again, and its new shoots will not fail" (Job 14:7).

Proverbs 11:11 teaches that God may even spare a society for the sake of a few godly people: "Through the blessing of the upright a city is exalted, but by the mouth of the wicked it is destroyed."

Abraham's urgent prayer for Sodom and Gomorrah (Gen. 18:6-33) demonstrates the significance that godly people can have in a godless society; God would have spared the cities, had He found ten righteous people in them (Gen. 18:32, 25).

In the end, our ungodly world is kept alive until the Second Coming of Christ because of the godly people still living in it, and because the kingdom of God is growing, as Jesus shows in the parable of the wheat and the tares (Mt. 13:24-30, 36-42). The tares are permitted to grow so that the wheat – the kingdom of God – will survive. When the wheat has matured and has filled the earth, the weeds will be destroyed.

As important as it is to analyse society's problems according to the Law of God, Christians have only one way to renew politics and society: "If my people, who are called by my name, will humble themselves and pray and seek my face and turn from their wicked ways, then will I hear from heaven and will forgive their sin and will heal their land" (2 Chr. 7:14). The church can then pray for society and for the state. Let us hope that God will not declare to us as He did to Ezekiel: "I looked for a man among them who would build up the wall and stand before me in the gap on behalf of the land so I would not have to destroy it, but I found none" (Ezek. 22:30).

Even when judgment seems inevitable, let us not spread panic, resignation and despair, but pray for our people as Abraham did.

Many have lost hope for Europe, because they see only signs of decline. Hope does not rely on visible reality, but reckons with God's intervention. When the first Christians brought hope to the Roman Empire, their situation was no better – on the contrary! Eastern Europe's recent history also reminds us that judgement can fall on antichristian powers in order to open the way for the Gospel!

51. Hope Is More Than Speculation

Proposition: Since Jesus clearly says that mankind cannot predict the day of His return, our actions must be determined by God's commandments, not by speculations about the future.

Jesus clearly forbids us to speculate about the day of His return: "He said to them: 'It is not for you to know the times or dates the Father has set by his own authority'" (Acts 1:7); "Therefore keep watch, because you do not know the day or the hour" (Mt. 25:13).

Nor have we any indication that any commandment can be nullified by reference to future events, even if we assume that we know exactly when they are to occur. God wants us to live according to His clearly revealed will, not according to future events, which He has deliberately concealed from us.

In the third chapter of 2 Timothy, Paul warns: "There will be terrible times in the last days" (2 Tim. 3:1), when "People will be lovers of themselves, lovers of money, boastful, proud, abusive, disobedient to their parents, ungrateful, unholy, without love, unforgiving, slanderous, without self-control, brutal, not lovers of the good, treacherous, rash, conceited, lovers of pleasure rather than lovers of God" (2 Tim. 3:2-4).

How is Timothy to live in such times? He is to follow Paul's teaching and his example (2 Tim. 3:10); he is to obey Scripture: "Evil men and impostors will go from bad to worse, deceiving and being deceived. But as for you, continue in what you have learned and have become convinced of, because you know those from whom you learned it, and how from infancy you have known the holy Scriptures, which are able to make you wise for salvation through faith in Christ Jesus. All Scripture is God-breathed and is useful for teaching, rebuking, correcting and training in righteousness, so that the man of God may be thoroughly equipped for every good work" (2 Tim. 3:13-17).

The only biblical rule for evil times is to keep the biblical commandments. Instead of prescribing special ethics for the Last Days, Scripture commands us to preach God's Word and to obey His commandments "in season and out of season" (2 Tim. 4:2). Above all, Paul exhorts Timothy: "Do the work of an evangelist" (2 Tim. 4:5). There is only one recipe for the Last Days, the Good News of the Gospel, that God offers us hope even at the darkest hour of our lives and gives us the prospect of a new beginning through reconciliation and forgiveness.

Hope for All Areas of Life

52. Reformation and Revival Mean Hope for the Church and for Society

Proposition: All reformations and revival movements have been driven by the hope of revival and renewal of the church and of society.

All of the **Reformers** of the sixteenth century advocated the separation of church and state, but at the same time encouraged society to consciously build on Christian values and precepts. They were convinced that God wants to thoroughly renew the church and the state as well as every individual. The idea that Luther, Calvin or any other of the Reformers were not interested in social issues, or that they had no hopes for this life, is absurd. All of them wanted to renew society as well as the church and worked for this goal by teaching people biblical values.

The fathers of **Pietism and the Revival Movements,** such as Philipp Jacob Spener, August Hermann Francke, Jonathan Edwards, John Wesley or George Whitefield, not only discovered personal conversion, but also, motivated by their own personal renewal, worked to influence both the church and society for the good of the poor and the weak. All were transformed by their hopes and were thus often denounced as revolutionaries.

Philipp Jakob Spener's Pietist reform program stimulated not only a flood of missionary activity, but also innumerable social institutions.[34] August Hermann Francke alone founded or encouraged the creation of numerous orphanages, schools for the poor, pharmacies and hospitals. His *Realschule* (Real school), a Pietist invention, provided children from poor or middle class families a "real" education designed to prepare them for the realities of life. Protestant cloisters[35] with their widespread aid to the poor, the el-

---

[34] See Helmuth Egelkraut. *Die Zukunftserwartung der pietistischen Väter.* Theologie und Dienst 53. Brunnen-Verlag: Gießen, 1987; Philipp Jacob Spener. *Umkehr in die Zukunft: Reformprogramm des Pietismus: Pia desideria.* ed. by Erich Beyreuther. Brunnen: Gießen, 1975²; See also Martin Schmidt. "Speners 'Pia Desideria': Versuch einer theologischen Interpretation", pp. 113-166 in: Martin Greschat (ed.). Zur neueren Pietismusforschung. Wege der Forschung CDXL. Wissenschaftliche Buchgesellschaft: Darmstadt, 1977.

[35] *Diakonissenmutterhäuser*: Protestant institutions somewhat like Roman Catholic cloisters, in which "deaconesses" vow to live in celibacy and to serve God.

derly and the sick, hospitals, homes for the aged, and, in more recent times, rehabilitation centres for drug addicts are all integral parts of Pietist history! Pietist leaders continually developed programs and lists of demands for state and society and published papers to educate both the state and its citizens about the meaning of Christian values for society.

The fathers of almost all Christian denominations – the Church Fathers; Lutheran Reformers such as Luther and Melanchthon; Reformed theologians such as Calvin, Bucer and Knox; Anglicans such as Cranmer; the fathers of Methodism, such as Wesley and Whitefield; and the Baptists (especially in the US and in England) assumed that Christians know righteous standards for society and will endeavour to realise their hopes through prayer, teaching, prophetic speaking, and action. The idea that Christians should completely withdraw from society, and that our personal hope has no consequences for society, is completely foreign to the confessions of any denomination!

European Christians must again begin to sow in hope, as the Reformers, Pietists, Revivalists and many others have done, and to work for distant goals, not only for the problems of the immediate future.

The individualism which has arisen in Europe and the West in the last 150 years has misled us to believe that our Christian faith is purely personal, that it has no social significance, and that it can even survive without fellowship in an organised church. This attitude engenders despair and robs Christians of hope. When we see no need to exert ourselves for others' sakes, we will soon lose hope for ourselves as well. This individualism, not the Bible, and not Pietism, has caused so many believers to withdraw from family life, from business, politics and science, and to give up testifying Christian values in everyday life.

53. Hope for the Weak

Proposition: Christian hope is especially directed towards the poor, the weak and the wretched, for "So the poor have hope" (Job 5:16), "but the needy will not always be forgotten, nor the hope of the afflicted ever perish" (Ps. 9:18). Innocent prisoners are "prisoners of hope" (Zech. 9:12), and the desolate widow "puts her hope in God and continues night and day to pray and to ask God for help" (1 Tim. 5:5).

European society has been strongly influenced by numerous groups such as the Salvation Army, Methodism, or the Protestant deaconesses, engaged in assistance of various social groups. We must renew our endeavours to help every individual, even if the rest of the world or even churches and other Christians have given him up, and offer him hope just as Jesus did.

54. Hope for All Cultures and Nations

Proposition: Christian hope offers hope for all cultures and for all nations. "In his name the nations will put their hope" (Mt. 21:21; see also Rom. 15:12). God is no respecter of persons (See Proposition 61). "(And for this we labour and strive), that we have put our hope in the living God, who is the Saviour of all men, and especially of those who believe" (1 Tim. 4:10).

Since God elected the Old Testament covenant people in order to provide hope for all peoples, world missions, the proclamation of hope for all, is central to the Old Testament. Abraham, Isaac and Jacob were called to be a blessing for all the nations of the earth (Gen. 12:3; 18:18; 22:17; 26:4; 28:14). The New Testament thus applies the promise given to the patriarchs to missions among non-Jews (Lk. 1:54-55,72; Acts 3:25-26; Rom. 4:13-25; Eph. 3:3-4; Gal. 3: 7-9,14; Heb. 6:13-20; 11:12).

The diversity of peoples and cultures is not the result of the Fall but was God's original intention. The Bible condemns no element of any culture that does not explicitly contradict God's holy will. Nor is the variety of cultures due to divine judgment over the Tower of Babel (Gen. 11:1-9). On the contrary, God confused the languages in order to fulfil His own commandment, the distribution of humanity over the whole earth ("fill the earth" Gen. 1:28; 9:1), which automatically leads to diversity of families and nations, but also of occupations, abilities and cultures. With the tower of Babel Satan intended to initiate a universal culture, his constant goal, as we see in the Book of Revelations and in the Antichrist. The "Beast," who receives his power from the "Dragon" (Rev. 13:1-10) "was given authority over every tribe, people, language and nation," but God wants neither a universal city nor universal Humanism. He and His Word alone, not any visible human institution, can guarantee the unity of the world. He scattered mankind over the face of the whole earth (Gen. 1:9), beginning with the sons of Noah populating the whole earth (Gen. 9:19) until the nations spread out over the whole earth (Gen. 10:5), which explains the origin of mankind from one genealogy (Gen. 10:1-32). God Himself is the Creator of the nations, for "from one man he made every nation of men, that they should inhabit the whole earth; and he determined the times set for them and the exact places where they should live" (Acts 17:26; see also Deut. 32:8; Ps. 74:17). Christians are thus free of any cultural straitjackets. No human traditions or rules bind us other than the Law of God. Mark 7:1-13 demonstrates this clearly when Jesus criticises the Pharisees, who have elevated their human culture to the level of divine law. Christians may judge other cultures according to biblical standards when they have learned to distinguish between their own culture (including their own religious culture) and the supraculturally valid Law of God. Again, Mark 7:1-13 is a good example. The Pharisees had honourable motives in creating extra regulations beside the Law of God and in imposing these rules on the rest of their society. Jesus criticises them, however, because in doing so, they had assumed the role of divine law-giver, equal to God: "They worship me in vain; their teachings are but rules taught by men" (Mk. 7:7: Mt. 15:9).

Because we belong to Christ alone and are subject to His Word alone, we can scrutinise both our own culture and the cultures of others, and are obliged by love to adapt to the culture of others. Paul justifies the necessity of adapting to others in evangelisation by referring to his liberty toward all men (1 Cor. 9:19-23). "Though I am free and belong to no man, I make myself a slave to everyone, to win as many as possible. To the Jews I became like a Jew, to win the Jews. To those under the law I became like one under the law (though I myself am not under the law), so as to win those under the law. To those not having the law I became like one not having the law (though I am not free from God's law but am under Christ's law), so as to win those not having the law. To the weak I became weak, to win the weak. I have become all things to all men so that by all possible means I might save some. I do all this for the sake of the gospel, that I may share in its blessings."

A Christian can thus live so intensely according to his own culture that he fails to notice that at best, he is being misunderstood, but, at worst, he is hindering others from understanding the gospel (1 Cor. 9:12). We are thus responsible, not only to tell others about salvation in Jesus Christ, but also to proclaim the gospel in a way that they can understand. For this reason, we can translate Scripture into any language imaginable and can – and must – express the gospel into every dialect and in every cultural form.

There is hope for Europe. Not that Europeans are closer to God or more important than other people. On the contrary, God loves all nations, even the Europeans, in spite of all that we have done in the past.

55. We Need to Express our Hope in Concrete Formulations for All Areas of Life and Creation

Proposition: Christian hope includes all Creation, both in its eternal fulfilment and also for the here and now. The final liberation of creation will encompass the entire living universe. "For the creation was subjected to frustration, not by its own choice, but by the will of the one who subjected it, in hope ..." (Rom. 8:20; see also verse 24). John's depiction of the new heaven and the new earth thus includes not only people but also the earth itself (We will discuss conservation in a later section.)

The Bible is concerned not only with the individual's private faith; it also addresses numerous social matters, such as the family, the economy, judicial, civil and organisational matters. Do such subjects as inheritance, child rearing, welfare, debts, inflation, bribery, salaries, taxes, prostitution, kidnapping, real estate, restitution, judges, kings, military spending, old ages pensions, self-defense, conservation, perjury, abortion, profit, the needs of the physically disabled, etc. concern individuals *alone*? I emphasise *alone* for, since all Christian ethical systems (and any transformation) begin with the life of the individual, any attempt to limit the Bible's significance to private life is doomed to fail. Scripture overflows with God's order of creation for mankind's collective existence. To reduce its laws to private matters equals the repudiation of God's commandments. As John Warwick Montgomery says, anyone who understands what Christianity really is, also automatically knows by definition that it expects its disciples to actively resist social evils and to make an effort to ease human need.[36]

In the following pages, I would like to discuss several areas of life: the family, the economy, law, politics and conservation. I hope that my ideas will encourage discussion on further issues and that experts in the various areas and professions will translate our appeal into their own terminology for their colleagues. One of Europe's greatest challenges is to find concrete formulations of biblical hope for everyday life in all areas of life, all profession and responsibilities.

---

[36] John Warwick Montgomery. *Christians in the Public Square. Law, Gospel and Public Policy.* Canadian Institute for Law, Theology and Public Policy: Edmonton (CAN), 1996,.p. 30.

Excursus: The Sources of Evangelical Ethics

Before discussing various aspects of social life, I would like to investigate the relationship between biblical hope, divine revelation in Scripture and human knowledge. Alister E. McGrath writes: "In general, Christian tradition has accepted four major sources: 1. Scripture, 2. Reason, 3. Tradition, 4. Experience."[37] Besides these sources, we could include ecclesiastical authority and the concrete situation and culture in which we find ourselves (all of which are included in McGrath's list).

For Evangelical ethics, the Word of God is the final and the only unassailable standard, the criterion for all other authorities (Latin: *norma normans*, i.e., the standard for all other standards). But what relative value do other sources such as ecclesiastical authority, reason, wisdom, experience or concrete situations and culture then have? Must they be rejected because the Bible has the highest authority? Or may they be consulted in ethical decisions? Tradition, experience and situation (or culture) are not the only sources for ethics, but merely classical denotations common to our civilisation, terminology we use to describe the way we receive good and right views of the world.

An exaggerated view more pious than that of Jesus or the apostles tries to ban these aspects from ethics. Claiming to be oriented only on the Bible, adherents of this approach reject any other standards or recommendations. This is, naturally, unrealistic. No one lives according to Scripture alone, and no one is incapable of distinguishing between good and evil in issues not explicitly handled in the Bible. We can find arguments against smoking, for example, even though Scripture doesn't speak of tobacco and smoking cannot be labelled "a sin." It is simply unhealthy, unsocial and unwise.

At this point, I would like to remind my readers that such an idea is completely foreign to the Bible, which repeatedly admonishes us to take the wisdom and experience of others seriously, to heed the warnings of the leaders of God's people or of other persons in authority, and to learn from history. Besides, the biblical writers also argue from experience or logic. If

---

[37] Alister E. McGrath. *Der Weg der christlichen Theologie.* C. H. Beck: München, 1997, p. 189; See the more detailed version in Ibid., pp. 189-243 (Ch. 6: "Die Quellen der Theologie"). Vernunft und Erfahrung neben der Schrift diskutiert Martin Honecker. *Einführung in die Theologische Ethik.* Walter de Gruyter: Berlin, 1990, pp. 187-202.

we consider the Bible to be our highest authority, we must also abide by its exhortation to accept advice, wisdom, experience, reason and the directions given by ecclesiastical or secular leaders. "This need to gain extrabiblical knowledge to understand the Bible is not an onerous necessity. It is a natural, normal part of our task, and God expects us to do it."[38]

God has indeed set several limits in His Word, but in doing so, has given us much greater freedom. Human thought, perverted under the curse of the Fall, can be a terrible tool in the hands of Satan, but as part of God's creative order intrinsic to the man as image of God, it is increasingly purified and transformed for God's purposes when the individual repents and turns to God. For this reason, Christians can be conscious, thinking people. Scripture provides us with an ethic of commandments, but also with an ethic of wisdom. Along with absolute regulations and limits, we are to learn from life experience and from wisdom, which judges the concrete situation properly and makes decisions which could be wrong in other situations. God created Man in cultural diversity and never intended us to all think, feel or work in the same ways.

Divine revelation must be the source of our thought, but it is not a substitute for thinking and planning. "The fear of the LORD is the beginning of wisdom" (Prov. 9:10; 7:1), not its end.

The ethics of 'Natural Law' thus has a certain validity for believers. As long as the Word of God determines our thinking, natural or situational ethics have a relative, non-absolute justification. The State needs some basic ethical foundation which includes the protection of human life. Given this ethical basis, it will then devise its traffic regulations and other laws from the nature of the matter. What happens at what speed, not divine revelation or Christian textbooks, will determine the speed limit.

One good example for the interplay of biblical knowledge and biblically based science can be found in the issue of abortion and birth control.[39] Not until biologists had discovered the merging of the male semen and the female egg, could we determine when human life begins. Ever since, Chris-

---

[38] John M. Frame. *The Doctrine of the Knowledge of God: A Theology of Lordship.* Presbyterian & Reformed: Phillipsburg (NJ), 1987, p. 67; See also pp. 66-68.

[39] See Richard M. Fagley. *The Population Explosion and Christian Responsibility.* Oxford University Press: New York, 1960, pp. 192-193.

tians insist that a person is a human being from the moment of conception and that any interruption of a pregnancy is homicide. At the same time, it was then possible to endorse certain forms of birth control, because no human life exists before conception, and because, in contrast to earlier ideas, preventing conception does not destroy human life.

Another example is child-rearing. Is it possible to raise children using only the Bible? Of course not – the Bible has nothing to say about health problems, about the amount of sleep children require, about forms of courtesy, about school ages or allowances. Scripture gives us God's purpose and general principles for child-rearing, which then distinguish biblical child-rearing from other forms. Parents are to "bring them up in the training and instruction of the Lord" (Eph. 6:4), to teach them to love God and His Word (2 Tim. 3:14-17) and to prepare them to live an independent life according to God's natural laws and under His authority. Beyond these general guidelines, the Bible contains only a few commandments or suggestions such as on corporal punishment or on the use of Bible stories (for example, on the Law: Deut. 4:9-10; 6:4-9, 20-25; 11:18-21; 31:12-13; 32:7; Josh. 4:6-7; Ps. 78:5-8; Prov. 22:7; about Passover: Ex. 12:26-27; 13:14-16. See also 13:6-10). Once parents have accepted the basic biblical injunction, they will naturally derive their methods from the 'nature of the thing.' The child's personal physical and mental development will determine many decisions and is often relatively comparable to those of other children – and the advice of non-Christians can be helpful!

Besides, Christian parents must translate these general principles into the realities of everyday life. In doing so, they apply to the experience of earlier generations (tradition), to modern advice, and to scientific studies, and use their discernment to find the best solution for their children, which is impossible for someone not familiar with the child's concrete situation. Final decisions require knowledge of the child's cultural background, the constellation of his family, and his environment.

God wishes and commands all men to employ the gifts they have received. Parents can encourage their children to do this only by observing them in order to discover their abilities and preferences, and by using their minds to develop concrete strategies.

Three dangers must be avoided. The first is to condemn outright any source of ethics or instruction beyond the Bible, which in reality only means that one is unaware of the influences that have formed one's own ideas. The second is to equate reasonable decisions or the experience of others with God's law, as when Christian writers prescribe supposedly infallible recipes, even though we all know that every child is different; parents with three children could easily write three completely different books! The third danger is to concentrate on reason and experience and ignore biblical orientation.

God has thus given us a basic goal for child-rearing, and the intelligence and wisdom to find the best method for our own children!

56. Biblical Hope in Opposition to the Deceptive Hope of Bourgeois Morality

Proposition: The Bible knows no neutral civil morality which makes work, industry, family, ownership or wealth, etc. absolute values, but only values which man, as a part of Creation, has received from God, and which he uses in gratitude and dependence on God.

The book of Ecclesiastes demonstrates this most clearly. Some have accused its writer of being a godless pessimist. R. B. Y. Scott concludes that he must have been a rationalist, an agnostic, a pessimist and a fatalist,[40] and that the ethical system of Ecclesiastes has no basis in divine commandments, for there are none.[41] Since the writer simply accepts his fate, all that is left to him is pleasure. The classical division of the book,[42] however, contradicts this view very clearly, for the repeated theme of the enjoyment of earthly life in 2:24-26; 5:17-19; 8:15-17; and 11:7-10 forms the conclusion of four major sections.[43] Each thus ends with the exhortation to enjoy life complete-

---

[40] R. B. Y. Scott. Proverbs, Ecclesiastes. *Anchor Bible.* Doubleday: Garden City (NY), 1965, p. 191. Scott does not intend his description to be a value judgment.

[41] Ibid., p. 192.

[42] See Walter C. Kaiser. Ecclesiastes: Total Life. *Everyman's Bible Commentary.* Moody Press: Chicago, 1979; and Addison G. Wright. "The Riddle of the Sphinx: The Structure of the Book of Qoheleth", pp. 45-66 in: Roy B. Zuck (ed.). *Reflecting with Solomon.* Baker Books: Grand Rapids (MI), 1994 [from Catholic Biblical Quarterly 30 (1968), pp. 313-334].

[43] Donald R. Glenn. "Der Prediger." pp. 651-696 in: John F. Walvoord, Roy F. Zuck (ed.). *Das Alte Testament erklärt und ausgelegt.* Vol. 2: 1. Könige-Hohelied. Hänssler: Neu-

ly and to live in the present, not in a distant future. "The negative images form the beginning, the positive ones the conclusion of each description."[44] The joys of life are expressly emphasised eight times (2:24-26; 3:11-14,22; 5:17-19; 8:15; 9:7-10; 11:7-10; see also 12:1). Words derived from the Hebrew root *smh* (joy, pleasure) appear seventeen times. Joy is the synopsis of the book. "A man can do nothing better than to eat and drink and find satisfaction in his work. This too, I see, is from the hand of God, for without him, who can eat or find enjoyment? To the man who pleases him, God gives wisdom, knowledge and happiness, but to the sinner he gives the task of gathering and storing up wealth to hand it over to the one who pleases God. This too is meaningless, a chasing after the wind" (Eccl. 2:24-26).

Recognising the Meaninglessness of Life Leads to Joy		
Section	What is meaningless	Exhortation to Joy
1:12-2, 26	Human Labour	2:24-26
3:1-15	The uncertainty of the future	3:12 (11-14)
3:16-22	Injustice in the world	3:22
5:9-19	Striving for wealth	5:17 (17-19)
8:10-15	Unpunished evil	8:15
9:1-10	The certainty of death	9:7-9
11:7-12:7	Old age and death	11:9-10; 12:1

How can the preacher move from pessimism to enjoyment so abruptly? Does he ignore the problems? No, he turns to God and realises that all is "from the hand of God" (2:24-26). Circumstances which seem meaningless and hopeless to man become meaningful when God, the Creator and Preserver, attracts our attention, and when we live a life pleasing to Him (2:26).

The purpose of Ecclesiastes is to point out the meaninglessness of labour, industry, family or possessions in themselves, without God, and to encour-

---

hausen, 1991. p. 655 (English original: *Bible Knowledge Commentary Old and New Testament,* here Ecclesiastes).

[44] Hans Möller. *Alttestamentliche Bibelkunde.* Lutherische Buchhandlung: Groß Oesingen, 1989. p. 194.

age mankind to receive these things as gifts from God, to use them under His guidance. As Donald R. Glenn has put it, Ecclesiastes expresses a valid criticism of modern secular humanism.[45] Without God, "who can eat or find enjoyment?" (2:25) "That everyone may eat and drink, and find satisfaction in all his toil – this is the gift of God" (3:13).

The idea of a neutral civil morality is not biblical. Things such as labour, industry, family, possessions, or wealth are not values in themselves, but have value only as gifts from the hand of God, which man can use in gratitude and dependence on Him. The Book of Ecclesiastes smashes the value system of civil morality, but it resurrects again under the Creator when it corresponds to God's commandments. When people come to a living faith in Christ, they cannot simply carry on with the same values as before, but must test them and let them be refined in the fire of Ecclesiastes, so that they are founded on God's Word and not on some civilised sense of "decency."

It is not our responsibility to understand everything, to have considered all possible consequences, and to comprehend the meaning of all things. Our responsibility is to live responsibly before God, to work, to enjoy and to form the world as we have received it from the Creator, for even the things that seem burdensome and meaningless to us have come from God. "I have seen the burden God has laid on men" (Eccl. 3:10).

Civil morality shatters when work, possessions, and family fail. For biblical morality, however, tragedy is not the end of life. Biblical morality offers hope not only for times of success and prosperity, as civil morality does, but its unlimited confidence in the Creator enables us to master suffering as well.

Ecclesiastes puts many biblical values into perspective – values which become dangerous when they take first place in our lives and replace God. The preacher warns, "The increase from the land is taken by all; the king himself profits from the fields. Whoever loves money never has money enough; whoever loves wealth is never satisfied with his income. This too is meaningless. As goods increase, so do those who consume them. And what benefit are they to the owner except to feast his eyes on them? The sleep of a labourer is sweet, whether he eats little or much, but the abundance of a rich man permits him no sleep" (5:10-12). Wealth can be positive and can be en-

---

[45] Donald R. Glenn. op. cit., p. 655.

joyed, but not when it becomes the goal of life, or suppresses or destroys the satisfaction given by labour. When things such as labour, family, possessions, or wisdom become the only goals, and life loses its eternal perspective, life loses its meaning. "All man's efforts are for his mouth, yet his appetite is never satisfied" (Prov. 6:7).

57. Hope for the Conservation of Creation[46]

Proposition: Conservationists have made the preservation of Creation into a political issue. Christians must remind them that there can be no creation without a Creator, and that hope for creation implies hope in the Creator.

Man's dominion over creation serves primarily human beings, but God intended it to serve the creation as well. Unlike the ungodly, anyone who keeps God's laws of creation will also serve creation. "A righteous man cares for the needs of his animal, but the kindest acts of the wicked are cruel" (Prov. 12:10). God gave Man the responsibility to "work" the world and to "take care of it" (Gen. 2:15), to change it and to preserve it. These two ideas seem to contradict each other, but in everyday life they are inseparable; they belong together like the two faces of a coin.

In a society moulded so strongly by Christianity, the modern conservationist movement attracts attention with its use of the word *creation,* at least in several European languages like German and French. Unfortunately, they misuse the term, because they deify nature and deny the difference between mankind and the rest of creation, instead of thinking in terms of the Creator. The Bible, on the other hand, teaches that man can preserve the earth only when he honours God and keeps God's laws. When Christians act to conserve the environment, they do it according to God's laws, not because nature has any sort of claim in itself. Christians must begin to fill the idea of preserving creation with Biblical content.

58. Hope for Society

Proposition: Although personal salvation is the first and most important goal of our hope and of missions, we may set other goals as well. All other goals gain their significance from the hope of personal salvation.

---

[46] See also Thomas Schirrmacher. *Eugen Drewermann und der Buddhismus.* VTR: Nürnberg, 2000[1]; 2001[2], pp. 71-116.

The Great Commission in Matthew 28:18-20 includes the exhortation to make disciples (learners). The first step in that direction is personal repentance – only individuals can be baptised – but as one individual after the other turns to Christ, whole nations are won. A high percentage of believers in a people does not contradict the notion of individual conversion.

Besides, conversion is not the end of renewal. The individual's new relationship to God is the beginning of renewal in himself, the family, the church, the economy, the state and society. All are to become disciples! Since Jesus tells his disciples to "make disciples of all nations ... teaching them to obey everything I have commanded you," the Great Commission means that Christians are to learn the entire spectrum of Biblical ethics, which will then transform the individual and his environment completely, so that, in the long run, sinful structures and visible injustice will be overcome.

The individual's peace with God, his personal salvation through Jesus' sacrifice of grace on the Cross, is mission's first and most important goal, which determines all subsequent aims. In Matthew 16:26 Jesus says very clearly that the salvation of the soul is more important than anything else. "What good will it be for a man if he gains the whole world, yet forfeits his soul? Or what can a man give in exchange for his soul?" Paul uses the same argument that both Jews and Greeks are lost in their sin, and that Jesus alone could achieve their salvation, before he introduces the subject of social, cultural and political ethics. "Therefore, since we have been justified through faith, we have peace with God through our Lord Jesus, through whom we have gained access by faith into this grace in which we now stand" (Rom. 5:1-2).

In the Sermon on the Mount, Jesus challenges Christians to let their light shine and to be the salt of the earth. Immediately after the Beatitudes, He uses these examples to show that believers do not live and work for themselves (Mt. 5:13-16). He admonishes us to act before and for others: "Let your light shine before men, that they may see your good deeds and praise your Father in heaven" (vs. 16).

In failing to actively pursue the welfare of our society, we accept the standards of our environment. No one can live without standards and values. If we do not actively endeavour to introduce Christian values into our world, or if we believe that our standards do not apply to society, we must find our values elsewhere – probably in our society. Klaus Bockmühl, professor of Ethics, once wrote, "The greatest danger for the 'lifeboat' or 'retreat' mentality is that its adherents continue to participate in the life of society unquestioningly and often with the greatest success. Finding it empty of divine guidance, they have no choice but to buy and sell according to the local rules, and surrender all the more to the domination of the 'Prince of this world'."[47]

59. Hope for the Family

Proposition: Missions and the message of hope begin in Christian churches and families, who teach the Word of God to the next generation through example, discipline, and education.

We dare not give up the proclamation of God's Word to the unchurched, but the Christian family must not be overlooked either, for a healthy Christian family is the requirement for leadership in the New Testament church (1 Tim. 3:4-5, 12-13; Tit. 1:6-7). When we relinquish our children to the state, we need not make any more effort to influence our churches, our economy, our society, or our state, for we have given up the best method of changing them for the future.

Raising our children is the most important step towards imparting hope and social politics, because we are preparing human beings for life, teaching them basic values and the principles of social contact. God created the family so that the younger generation can learn biblical standards for the welfare of the whole society from their adult role models. Where else are people to learn to be considerate, not to envy, to help the weak or to praise others, if not at home? Let's not retreat from the areas of life that God has placed in our hands! Let us use the opportunities we have to influence education by founding Christian schools and by supporting Christian teachers in state schools.

Healthy families and Christian families are possible only as long as we ensure that the areas left to us by society and the State are kept intact. If we want to preserve the family, we must support the efforts of Christians to influence our society, for our society determines to a large extent what the family can do. The destruction of the family is driven by social forces, which can only be resisted when families begin to influence society for their own good. The attempts of Communist states to destroy the Christian family speak for themselves.

---

[47] Klaus Bockmühl. *Theologie und Lebensführung: Gesammelte Aufsätze II.* TVG. Brunnen: Gießen, 1982, p. 131.

The modern family is losing its authority and its most important functions with only fragments of its earlier responsibilities for the economy, education, and the welfare of society remaining. As the family abandons its essential roles, the workplace has been removed from the home; nonmarital sexual relationships are being equated with marriage; the elderly, the ill and the disabled are segregated into 'homes.' Only when Christian values are re-vived, can family life and family responsibility again develop.

60. Hope for the Economy

Proposition: Since we were created with the need for hope to motivate our labour and our economic endeavours, our visions of the future largely determine our economic ethics.

Speaking of his missionary work, Paul wrote, "(and for this we labour and strive), that we have put our hope in the living God, who is the Saviour of all men, and especially of those who believe" (1 Tim. 4:10) and "When the plowman plows and the thresher threshes, they ought to do so in the hope of sharing in the harvest" (1 Cor. 9:10). Since missions is only one aspect of labour, he applies the same principles to the duties of the elders (1 Tim. 5:17-20; 1 Cor. 9:9-18).

Although many Christians fail to understand the extensive social conse-quences of some biblical/Christian commandments, secular analysts realise that biblical principles have quite practical effects on the economy. Helmut Schoeck, professor of Sociology, writing on the Biblical condemnation of en-vy in the Ten Commandments and in the words of Jesus, says, "The New Testament speaks almost always to the envious individual, and admonishes him to bear the disparity between himself and his neighbour with maturity and like a Christian. In Western society Christian ethics have protected and encouraged man's creative energies, and have made the extent of its achievements possible by constraining covetousness."[48] Those who nourish envy surrender an essential teaching of the Christian faith and transform so-ciety into a horrible battlefield.

---

[48] Helmut Schoeck. *Der Neid und die Gesellschaft.* Ullstein: Frankfurt, 1987[6].

61. Hope for the Legal System

Proposition: Christian hope for God's comprehensive, incorruptible judgement encourages us to seek truth and justice here on earth, even though it can only be incomplete and is constantly threatened by wickedness and by human limitations.

Hope is always based on the expectation of justice, but without God, we learn from experience: "We look for justice, but find none; for deliverance" (Isa. 59:11). The believer knows, however, that "But by faith we eagerly await through the Spirit the righteousness for which we hope" (Gal. 5:5). However we interpret the Bible's teachings on the Last Judgement, whether we believe that justice will or even can be expected before that or not, any search for justice finds its significance and its dignity here.

The roots of the constitutional state lie in a variety of philosophical ideas, but its primary basis is the Scriptural doctrine of law. Any denial of this foundation submits justice to caprice.

The basic civil right to a fair process of law is an ancient principle found in both the Old and the New Testaments. The definition of law requires a just judge, and God is the prototype (See, for example, Deut. 10:17-18; Ps. 7:9,12; 9:5; 50:6; 58:2-3; Ps. 75:3, 8). A fair judge is always acting in God's commission (2 Chr. 19:6-7). The magistrate must realise that God sees him and is on the side of the innocent: "To deny a man his rights before the Most High, to deprive a man of justice – would not the Lord see such things?" (Lam. 3:35-36)

A verdict must be made without partiality (Deut. 1:17; 2 Chr. 19:7; Prov. 18:5; 24:23; Job 13:10; Col. 3:25; Eph. 6:9), for God is impartial (for example, Deut. 19:17-18). Only wicked judges practise partiality (Isa. 3:9). Prejudice must not influence the verdict (1 Tim. 5:21), and the case must be investigated thoroughly (See, for example, Deut. 17:4).

Scripture thus forbids any legal double standard, such as one law for the nobility and another for the peasants. Even foreigners enjoyed the same legal rights as the Israelites under Old Testament law (Ex. 12:49). "Do not pervert justice; do not show partiality to the poor or favouritism to the great, but judge your neighbour fairly" (Lev. 19:15). God defends the rights of the poor and the destitute (Prov. 29:7; 31:8). In fact, the Bible assesses the justice of a nation by its treatment of the weak. The welfare of the ruling parties is no more significant than the condition of the helpless. Scripture does not judge by the state of the wealthy, who have money and the power to defend their rights, but by the situation of the poor, the widows, and the orphans in the legal system. "Speak up for those who cannot speak for themselves, for the rights of all who are destitute. Speak up and judge fairly; defend the rights of the poor and needy" (Prov. 31:8-9). God, the Creator and Lord of mankind, wishes us to treat each other like images of God and like created beings, not like animals.

There can be no justice without law, and without justice no state can please God. Not until the modern age, a period of history moulded by Christian, biblical principles, were the mighty of the earth subjected to the law and to justice. The days when a king could claim, "I am the State!"[49] are fortunately over. Even the highest state officials, even the state itself, are subject to law, must obey the law, and can be sued and condemned when they do not. As Christians we have an important role to play, for without justice power becomes despotism. "Righteousness exalts a nation, but sin is a disgrace to any people" (Prov. 24:34). The Church Father St. Augustine wrote, "What is the State but a gang of thieves, if there is no law? Gangs of thieves are nothing but small states."[50] He illustrates his proposition with a clear example; asked by Alexander the Great how he dared to make the sea so dangerous, a pirate replied defiantly, "Just because I use a small ship you call me a robber. You do it with a fleet and call yourself emperor."[51]

As long as we deny the archetype of our impartial God, corruption and bribery will increase in Europe. Only few realise that this is the logical consequence of our surrender of Christian principles. "A wicked man accepts a bribe in secret to pervert the course of justice" (Prov. 17:23). In turning our

---

[49] On Sept 7,1891, Kaiser Wilhelm II, in his boundless vanity, signed the Golden Book of the City of Munich with the words, "Suprema lex regis voluntas," ("The hightest law is the will of the king"). Gerhard Jaeckel. Die deutschen Kaiser. Weltbild-Verlag: Augsburg, n. d. (Repr. of Urbes-Verlag: Gräfeling), p. 188. The entry can be seen in Hans-Michael Körner. "'Na warte Wittelsbach!': Kaiser Wilhelm II. und das Königreich Bayern", pp. 31-42 in: Hans Wilderotter, Klaus-D. Pohl (ed.). Der letzte Kaiser: Wilhelm II. im Exil. Bertelsmann Lexikon Verlag: Gütersloh & Deutsches Historisches Museum Berlin, 1991, p. 37.

[50] Aurelius Augustinus. Vom Gottesstaat. Bd. 1. dtv-klassik. dtv: München, 1988³. p. 173 (Kapitel 4 "Reiche ohne Gerechtigkeit sind große Räuberbanden" in Buch 4).

[51] Ibid., p. 174.

back on God, we give up the archetype of the fair judge, whose absolute justice and integrity are the basis for any rejection of the perversion of justice. Doesn't the Old Testament continually describe Him as "the great God, mighty and awesome, who shows no partiality and accepts no bribes" (Deut. 10:17)? "Now let the fear of the LORD be upon you. Judge carefully, for with the LORD our God there is no injustice or partiality or bribery" (2 Chr. 19:7).

It was an Evangelical Christian, inspired by his Christian hope, who uncovered the corruption rampant in the EC and forced the Commission to resign. Here we can see the immense consequences that honesty and biblical values in small things can have. His book on the experience is called 'Integrity for Europe'![52] What a program! A drop in a bucket can be the beginning of an ocean!

62. Hope for Politicians

Proposition: Godly men in the Bible often held important positions as officials or rulers in their governments – why not in Europe?

Scripture tells us of many godly judges, kings, and officials in Israel as well as in other states. God made Joseph the most powerful man in Egypt after Pharaoh and placed Daniel in high office in several empires. As queen, Esther was influential in the Persian empire, and Nehemiah served as governor under a heathen ruler. Nebuchadnezzar, king of Babylon, was converted; the king of Nineveh repented on hearing Jonah's message. Naaman, the right hand of the king of Syria, was converted by an Israelite maid and the prophet Elisha. All of these people retained their offices after their conversion. The New Testament tells us of numerous Roman soldiers and officers (for example, Mt. 8:5-13; 15:39; 27:54; Lk. 7:2-9; 23:47; Acts 10:1-48) and of Dionysius (Acts 17:34), the mayor of Athens, who all became Christians, but did not have to surrender their offices as a result.

The New Testament provides the Christian officials of its day with clear, just precepts for their duties as tax collectors, soldiers, or policemen. John the Baptist, for example, advises Roman officials: "Tax collectors also came to be

---

[52] Paul van Buitenen. *Blowing the Whistle: Fraud in the European Commission*. Politico's Publ.: London, 2000; German: Paul van Buitenen. *Unbestechlich für Europa: Ein EU-Beamter kämpft gegen Mißwirtschaft und Korruption*. Brunnen: Gießen, 1999.

baptized. 'Teacher,' they asked, 'what should we do?' 'Don't collect any more than you are required to,' he told them. Then some soldiers asked him, 'And what should we do?' He replied, 'Don't extort money and don't accuse people falsely – be content with your pay'" (Lk. 3:12-14; see also Lk. 7:29). After his conversion, Zacchaeus, the tax collector, reimbursed the people he had cheated (Lk. 19:1-10): "But Zacchaeus stood up and said to the Lord, 'Look, Lord! Here and now I give half of my possessions to the poor, and if I have cheated anybody out of anything, I will pay back four times the amount'" (Lk. 19:8; see also Ex. 22:1).

Many Christians consider politics wicked by definition, but why be surprised that it is such a 'dirty' business when we fail to participate. Why should politicians be interested in God's standards when the Church encourages them to ignore them? As a matter of fact, even a good policy is a 'dirty' business, because politics' most important responsibility is to fight crime and wickedness. If God has given authority to the State, it cannot be fundamentally wrong, just as parental authority is not basically wrong, even though ungodly parents misuse their power. Politics do not destroy character; they reveal it. If all godly people withdraw from political life, we can only expect the ungodly to take their places.

We must learn that, although God intended church and state to be two separate institutions, both have their divinely appointed responsibilities, and the values preached by the church and ordained by God are valid for all of creation. Individual Christians make policies, not as representatives of the church, but as citizens. The church's duty is to teach godly principles to the government without forcing its ideas on the state or taking it over.

63. Hope for Peace

Proposition: Hope for visible peace in small matters and in major affairs grows from the invisible peace with God, for God wills a future in peace.
"'For I know the plans I have for you,' declares the LORD, 'plans to prosper you and not to harm you, plans to give you hope and a future'" (Jer. 29:11).

The individual's relationship to God determines his personal morality as well as his social ethics. In Romans Paul first demonstrates the lost condition of both Jews and Greeks and the necessity of salvation in Christ. In Chapter 5 he writes, "Therefore, since we have been justified through faith, we have peace with God through our Lord Jesus Christ, through whom we have gained access by faith into this grace in which we now stand. And we rejoice in the hope of the glory of God" (Rom. 5:1-2). Only then does he begin to discuss personal (Rom. 6-8), cultural (14-15) and political (13:1-7) ethics. The book of Romans shows that our very personal faith has consequences for concrete issues of daily life such as work, the nation, and the state. We cannot limit faith to our personal relationship to God and to the church without cutting out large sections of the book of Romans!

Since "fights and quarrels," including conflicts between believers, come from our desires (Jas. 4:1-2), from our inner being, the only defence against them must come from within, from peace with God and with our fellow men. This peace, which begins in our hearts, must flow into our lives and fill it completely.

64. Hope Requires Dialogue, not Violence

Proposition: Hope gives us the serenity to discuss issues with those who advocate different positions.

Dialogue, the peaceful discussion, patient and honest listening, and learning from others is a Christian virtue, but we cannot surrender Christianity's absolute claim to truth or its responsibility for world missions without disintegrating our faith altogether.

A dialogue between Christians and the adherents of other religions and worldviews is possible to the extent that we can discuss our faith in a peaceful manner ("Always be prepared to give an answer to everyone who asks you to give the reason for the hope that you have. But do this with gentleness and respect" – 1 Pet. 2:15-16), that we listen to others (Jas. 1:19), that we are willing to learn from others' experience in many areas of life (See Proverbs), and that we are always prepared to examine ourselves and our behaviour.

Dialogue which requires even temporarily or theoretically denying the absolute truth of Jesus Christ's central claim (Jn. 14:6), of the gospel (Rom. 1:16-17; 2:16), or the Word of God (2 Tim. 3:16-17; Heb. 4:12-13; Jn. 17:17); or the equation of Scriptural revelation with the Scriptures of other religions; is completely incompatible with Christian missions and with the very nature of Christianity. The Bible's claim to absolute authority is most clearly expressed in the doctrines of the Last Judgement and Eternal Life. Hebrew 6:1-2 lists "the resurrection of the dead, and eternal judgment," under the six essential foundations of our faith. The Church has upheld these concepts throughout her history as the Apostolic Creed reminds us: *"from thence he shall come to judge the quick and the dead."*

65. Hope for Churches

Proposition: Only churches who have hope for themselves can offer hope to Europe. We need leaders who practice and teach hope.

We must remember that God wills church growth, both as external church planting and as internal maturity; growth in numbers and spiritual growth in the deep, personal love to God, to His Word and in the hope based on His limitless possibilities.

So many European churches have resigned themselves to the secularisation and esoterisation of our society. Many church leaders continue to sacrifice themselves in service, but have no perspective for the future. They administrate the state of affairs they have inherited, but have no message for the future and no vision of God's possibilities.

Europe needs leaders with hope. We must relinquish our intellectual, philosophical and theoretical theological training educational system and develop a new, vibrant, training program such as those used by Jesus or Paul. We need preparation which transforms practice by transforming thought and which confronts the relevant issues of our day. Only those who have real hope can teach it to a new generation of leaders.[53]

66. There Is Hope for Politics When the Church Repents

Proposition: Beginning with the biblical-reformational renewal of the individual, and moving forward through the renewal of the family, the Christian church must first begin to renew the Reformation.

---

[53] See Thomas Schirrmacher. "Jesus as Master Educator and Trainer," *Training for Crosscultural Ministries* (World Evangelical Fellowship) 2/2000: pp 1-4; "Paul and His Colleagues." *Training for Crosscultural Ministries* (World Evangelical Fellowship) 3/2000: pp 6-8; "Ausbilden wie Jesus und Paulus," pp. 7-43 in Klaus W. Müller, Thomas Schirrmacher (Hg.). Ausbildung als missionarischer Auftrag. Referate der Jahrestagung 1999 des afem. edition afem – mission reports 7. Verlag für Kultur und Wissenschaft: Bonn, 1999.

"For it is time for judgment to begin with the family of God" (1 Pet. 4:17),[54] for Paul's remark about the Jews, which agrees with the Old Testament, is just as valid for the Church: "As it is written: 'God's name is blasphemed among the Gentiles because of you'" (Rom. 2:24). The sins of Christians and of the church are worse than those of the 'world': "If they have escaped the corruption of the world by knowing our Lord and Saviour Jesus Christ and are again entangled in it and overcome, they are worse off at the end than they were at the beginning. It would have been better for them not to have known the way of righteousness, than to have known it and then to turn their backs on the sacred command that was passed on to them" (2 Pet. 2:20, 21).

Let us repeat: there is only one way to renew politics and our society. As important as it is to search the Law of God to determine what is going wrong and to rediscover God's way of doing things, we must begin with ourselves: "If my people, who are called by my name, will humble themselves and pray and seek my face and turn from their wicked ways, then will I hear from heaven and will forgive their sin and will heal their land." (2 Chr. 7:14). Then we can begin to truly pray for our society and our governments. Let us hope that God will not say the same thing about us that He said about Israel: "I looked for a man among them who would build up the wall and stand before me in the gap on behalf of the land so I would not have to destroy it, but I found none" (Ezek. 22:30). "The authentic gospel must become visible in the transformed lives of men and women. As we proclaim the love of God we must be involved in loving service, as we preach the Kingdom of God we must be committed to its demands of justice and peace."[55]

May the God of hope fill you with all joy and peace as you trust in him, so that you may overflow with hope by the power of the Holy Spirit. (Romans 15:13)

---

[54] John Calvin emphasises this idea particularly. See Heinrich Berger. *Calvins Geschichtsauffassung. Studien zur Dogmengeschichte und Systematischen Theologie 6.* Zwingli-Verlag: Zürich, 1956, p. 229.

[55] *Das Manifest von Manila.* Lausanner Bewegung – Deutscher Zweig: Stuttgart, 1996, p. 14 (paragraph 4); English text: www.gospelcom.net/lcwe/statements manila.html (26.11.2001).

The Author

Bishop Prof. Dr. theol. Dr. phil. Thomas Schirrmacher, PhD, ThD, DD, serves the World Evangelical Alliance as Associate Secretary General for Theological Concerns (Theology, Theological Education, Intrafaith Relations, Interfaith Relations, Religious Freedom, Global Scholars) and as Chair of the Theological Commission. He is also chair of the same commission of the European Evangelical Alliance. As President of the International Council of the International Society for Human Rights and as director of the International Institute for Religious Freedom (Bonn, Cape Town, Colombo, Brasilia), he regularly testifies in the parliaments and courts in Europe and the Americas, the OSCE and the UN in Geneva and New York. His has authored and edited 102 books, his newest including 'Fundamentalism', 'Racism', 'Human Rights', 'Suppressed Women', and 'Human Trafficking'.

Schirrmacher earned four doctorates in Ecumenical Theology, in Cultural Anthropology, in Ethics and in the Sociology of Religion and received two honorary doctorates from the USA and India. He teaches as Extraordinary Professor of the Sociology of Religion at the state University of the West in Timişoara (Romania) and at the University of Oxford (Regent's Park College). He is also president of Martin Bucer European Theological Seminary and Research Institutes (with branches in Berlin, Bielefeld, Bonn, Chemnitz, Dehli, Hamburg, Helsinki, Innsbruck, Istanbul, Izmir, Linz, Munich, Pforzheim, Prague, Sao Paulo, Tirana, Zurich).

Giving Hands

GIVING HANDS GERMANY (GH) was established in 1995 and is officially recognized as a nonprofit foreign aid organization. It is an international operating charity that – up to now – has been supporting projects in more than 40 countries on four continents. In particular we care for orphans and street children. Our major focus is on Africa and Central America. GIVING HANDS always mainly provides assistance for self-help and furthers human rights thinking.

The charity itself is not bound to any church, but on the spot we are cooperating with churches of all denominations. Naturally we also cooperate with other charities as well as governmental organizations to provide assistance as effective as possible under the given circumstances.

The work of GIVING HANDS GERMANY is controlled by a supervisory board. Members of this board are Colonel V. Doner, Kathleen McCall, and Wendy Swezy. Dr. Christine Schirrmacher is registered as legal manager of GIVING HANDS at the local district court. The local office and work of the charity are coordinated by Rev. Horst J. Kreie as executive manager. Prof. Dr. Thomas Schirrmacher serves as a special consultant for all projects.

Thanks to our international contacts companies and organizations from many countries time and again provide containers with gifts in kind which we send to the different destinations where these goods help to satisfy elementary needs. This statutory purpose is put into practice by granting nutrition, clothing, education, construction and maintenance of training centers at home and abroad, construction of wells and operation of water treatment systems, guidance for self-help and transportation of goods and gifts to areas and countries where needy people live.

GIVING HANDS has a publishing arm under the leadership of Titus Vogt, that publishes human rights and other books in English, Spanish, Swahili and other languages.

These aims are aspired to the glory of the Lord on the basis of the Holy Bible according to the Apostles' Creed as well as the Universal Declaration of Human Rights (1948).

Baumschulallee 3a · D-53115 Bonn · Germany
Phone: +49 / 228 / 695531 · Fax +49 / 228 / 695532
www.gebende-haende.de · info@gebende-haende.de

Martin Bucer Seminary

Faithful to biblical truth
Cooperating with the Evangelical Alliance
Reformed

Solid training for the Kingdom of God

- Alternative theological education
- Study while serving a church or working another job
- Enables students to remain in their own churches
- Encourages independent thinking
- Learning from the growth of the universal church.

Academic

- For the Bachelor's degree: 180 Bologna-Credits
- For the Master's degree: 120 additional Credits
- Both old and new teaching methods: All day seminars, independent study, term papers, etc.

Our Orientation:

- Complete trust in the reliability of the Bible
- Building on reformation theology
- Based on the confession of the German Evangelical Alliance
- Open for innovations in the Kingdom of God

Our Emphasis:

- The Bible
- Ethics and Basic Theology
- Missions
- The Church

Our Style:

- Innovative
- Relevant to society
- International
- Research oriented
- Interdisciplinary

Structure

- 15 study centers in 7 countries with local partners
- 5 research institutes
- President: Prof. Dr. Thomas Schirrmacher
  Vice President: Prof. Dr. Thomas K. Johnson
- Deans: Thomas Kinker, Th.D.;
  Titus Vogt, lic. theol., Carsten Friedrich, M.Th.

Missions through research

- Institute for Religious Freedom
- Institute for Islamic Studies
- Institute for Life and Family Studies
- Institute for Crisis, Dying, and Grief
  Counseling
- Institute for Pastoral Care

Europe:
Restoring Hope

Deborah Meroff

The continent known for over 1000 years as the heartland of Christianity has gone into spiritual arrest. Drawing from the experience of many individuals and organisations, this book takes a hard look at four population groups at the centre of Europe's heart trouble: marginalised people, Muslims, youth and nominal and secular Europeans. Here is proof that it is possible to restore hope to this great continent when God's people work together. This practical resource supplies all the motivation and information we need to get started.

"Europe is very likely a battleground for the future of global Christianity... I hope that whoever reads these pages will be encouraged and inspired to prayer and action."

Jiří Unger
Former President of the European Evangelical Alliance

"My wife Drena and I have now been based in Europe for 50 years. Debbie Meroff's book True Grit was one of the most important books in our lives, and her new book on Europe is another cutting edge, must-read!"

George Verwer
Founder and International Co-ordinator Emeritus, OM International

"This book shows that God is still at work in Europe. He is building his church despite many challenges. And he wants to see each one of us playing an active part in restoring hope to Europe!"

Frank Hinkelmann
President of the European Evangelical Alliance

Pb. • pp. 296 • £ 14.95 • US$ 24.95 • € 14.95
ISBN 978-3-941750-06-7

VTR Publications • Gogolstr. 33 • 90475 Nürnberg • Germany
info@vtr-online.com • http://www.vtr-online.com

The Heart of Church and Mission

Bryan Knell

This book brings together a passion for the church and a passion for global mission. It looks at the heart of the UK church, asking whether and how it beats for mission and explores the passion of the mission community, and asks how it involves the local church. You might be forgiven for expecting that the heart of church and the heart of mission would be interwoven and closely linked together, but that has not been the case.

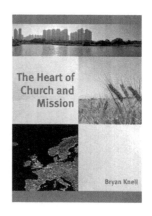

Two significant historical events continue to shape the church and mission in the Western World. Christendom removed mission from the church and the launch of the missionary societies disengaged the local church from mission. Although there is plenty of talk of change, the dominant mind-set is still shaped by these events. Practical suggestions are directed at churches and agencies with the aim of re-establishing, Mission at the heart of the church and the church at the heart of mission.

The world is a different place to when the "modern" Western mission movement developed. Yet many of the same structures exist today, in both churches and mission agencies. The church in the West needs to engage in new and appropriate ways in the world, building on history but not being bound by it. Bryan's prophetic call is to new ways of thinking, new attitudes and clear Biblical principles and deserves a wide audience. The Global Church deserves no less than a fresh approach to obeying His command to join together in God's mission in His world.

Martin Lee, Executive Director, Global Connections, UK

Pb. • pp. 80 • £ 6.00 • US$ 9.99 • € 9.95
ISBN 978-3-95776-037-1

VTR Publications • Gogolstr. 33 • 90475 Nürnberg • Germany
info@vtr-online.com • http://www.vtr-online.com

Evangelism
in Europe

Hannes Wiher (ed.)

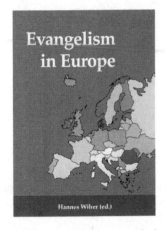

To think Europe represents a challenge. A challenge that may seem foolish to take up, but which corresponds to a reality. Some great personalities accepted this challenge, just after World War II. It was really necessary to do something! As regards missiology, it took more than a half century to confront the task. It is time to meet our responsibilities. The gravity and extreme complexity of this challenge call for a deep awareness of the situation in Europe, an analysis of contemporary practices, a theological reflection on the spiritual condition of Europeans, the witness of old and new churches, and the nature of the Gospel that has to be announced.

Profiting from an overview of Europe, we are at the same time aware of the particularities that each country presents. The commonalities and the differences will both shape the evangelistic approach adopted in each European country. Looking at the whole of Europe, we will also become more conscious of Europe's specific challenges and opportunities.

This is a considerable enterprise. Many have been engaged in it recently. The Network of evangelical missiologists in French speaking Europe (REMEEF) wants to make its modest contribution. It hopes that this book will be an encouraging read and provide the tools and innovative ideas for those eager to be Daniels and Calebs for our fellow Europeans.

With contributions from Hannes Wiher, Neal Blough, Julien Coffinet, Evert van de Poll, David Brown, Johannes Müller, and Léo Lehmann. Preface by Bernard Huck.

Pb. • pp. viii/352 • £ 20.00 • US$ 25.00 • € 20.00
ISBN 978-3-95776-081-4

VTR Publications • Gogolstr. 33 • 90475 Nürnberg • Germany
info@vtr-online.com • http://www.vtr-online.com

Bert de Ruiter (ed.)

Engaging with Muslims in Europe

In Europe one finds Christian communities and Muslim communities living in close proximity to each other. Muslims and Christians pass each other in the streets, stand next to each other waiting for the bus or metro, live next to one another in streets, share apartment buildings with each other, study in the same universities, have their lunches in the same business canteens, shop in the same shopping centres. Nevertheless, they are essentially strangers to each other. Only a small minority of Churches and Christians in Europe are engaged with Muslims through meaningful and loving relationships which provide opportunities to witness to them about the truth of God.

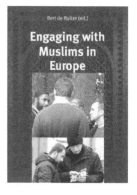

The European Ministry to Muslims Network of the European Leadership Forum seeks to equip the Church in Europe to relate to Muslims with a compassionate heart, an informed mind, an involved hand and a witnessing tongue. In this book members of the network and others write about their engagement with Muslims in Europe.

Pb. • pp. 112 • £ 7.00 • $ 12.00 • € 8.00
ISBN 978-3-95776-025-8

VTR Publications • Gogolstr. 33 • 90475 Nürnberg • Germany
info@vtr-online.com • http://www.vtr-online.com